"This charming, tremendously personal book speaks so beautifully of the remote and glorious land it comes from, and is packed with wonderful 'perfectly imperfect' tales of life, cooking, and the love of place."

—SUZANNE GOIN

"I was hooked by Erin French's charming storytelling. Home cooks will enjoy the warm tone in which Erin has written her recipes. They are a breeze to follow, call for only a handful of mostly easy-to-find ingredients, and reveal the good life of the four seasons in Maine."

—NANCY SILVERTON

"One of the most magical experiences of my life was eating at Erin French's Lost Kitchen . . . The food was deeply personal, local, and delicious. I am filled with joy at the prospect of re-creating some of the dishes at home from the recipes in this gorgeous cookbook."

—DANA COWIN

THE
# LOST KITCHEN

CLARKSON POTTER/PUBLISHERS
NEW YORK

THE

# LOST KITCHEN

RECIPES AND A GOOD LIFE FOUND IN FREEDOM, MAINE

———

ERIN FRENCH

WITH RACHEL HOLTZMAN

PHOTOGRAPHS BY NICOLE FRANZEN

Published in the United States by Clarkson Potter/Publishers,
an imprint of the Crown Publishing Group, a division of
Penguin Random House LLC, New York.
crownpublishing.com
clarksonpotter.com

CLARKSON POTTER is a trademark and POTTER with
colophon is a registered trademark of Penguin Random
House LLC.

Library of Congress Cataloging-in-Publication Data

Names: French, Erin, Chef author.
Title: The lost kitchen : recipes and a life found in Freedom,
Maine / Erin French.
Description: First edition. | New York : Clarkson Potter/
Publishers, [2017] | Includes index.
Identifiers: LCCN 2016004581 (print) | LCCN 2016014613
(ebook) | ISBN 9780553448436 (hardcover) | ISBN
9780553448443 (eISBN) | ISBN 9780553448443 (ebook)
Subjects: LCSH: Cooking, American--New England style.
| Cooking--Maine--Freedom. | Seasonal cooking. | LCGFT:
Cookbooks.
Classification: LCC TX715.2.N48 F735 2017 (print) | LCC
TX715.2.N48 (ebook) | DDC 641.5974--dc23
LC record available at http://lccn.loc.gov/2016004581

ISBN 978-0-553-44843-6
eISBN 978-0-553-44844-3

Printed in China

Book and cover design by Danielle Deschenes
Cover photography by Nicole Franzen
Endpaper art by Shutterstock © swinner

10

First Edition

FOR MY MUM

Who taught me to pay attention
to my surroundings, follow my
heart, and never give up. You are
the fletch to my arrow.

# CONTENTS

————

OPPOSITE: SKILLET MUSSELS with Rosemary, Lavender & Lime, *page 107*

# THE LOST KITCHEN,

S ixteen miles west of the midcoast Maine town of Belfast lies a rural village called Freedom. Drive inland along Route 137, leaving behind the salty breezes of Penobscot Bay, and you pass little ponds, farmland, and wooded lanes. A singular flashing traffic light (the only one for miles) signals that you are nearly there. Once you've driven by the tractor shop, convenience store, and little diner on the corner and descended the hill into the heart of the tiny village below, you've found Freedom: population 719.

This is my home. It was on the back dirt roads of Freedom that I first rode a bike and at Sandy Pond where I learned to swim and ice fish and skate. It was along the old network of hiking trails where I discovered a love for nature and, in the soil of my family's farm, the magic of growing things. I sold eggs by the roadside with my sister and made mud dams in the streams with the farm boys next door, and battled potato bugs, armed with a Mason jar filled with a couple fingers of gasoline.

Growing up in rural Maine, I came to understand the value of a home-cooked meal, the joy of gathering around a supper table, and the importance of timeless dishes that form the fabric and culture of this place. I first noticed the simple pleasures of whole foods through the taste of fresh green beans, the cool and prickly crunch of a baby cucumber, the smell of a perfectly ripe tomato, the treasure hunt of digging for new potatoes.

As I grew older I found my place at the stove in my family's fifty-seat restaurant, a rural greasy-spoon diner that my father owned for twenty years. By age fourteen I had learned how to cook fish to perfection, get a hamburger to a nice pink medium-rare, and run the lunch and dinner line between soccer practice and book reports. I was my dad's replacement, giving him a break from a grueling sixteen-hour workday. He could finally lounge on the back deck of the restaurant with his friends, drink a beer, and sometimes use the cornfield in the distance as a golf driving range while inside I prepared platters of perfectly fried clams with mayo laced with diced bread-and-butter pickles. Occasionally I made a few extra bucks retrieving golf balls; after a few beers, my dad's friends would gladly pay me a dollar a ball.

By sixteen I was seriously cooking on the line. It was hard work, but it paid (I was one of the only kids in school who could afford her own car, a 1984 VW Rabbit), and I found pleasure in cooking—especially when Dad wasn't around and I was the boss. I created evening specials, garnished the lobster rolls with nasturtiums and violets I had harvested from my mother's garden, and played around with desserts like tart rhubarb crisp with buttermilk ice cream—even though the locals seemed to prefer the graham cracker pie and instant chocolate pudding with aerosol whipped cream. I sometimes snuck a bag of brightly colored mixed baby lettuces into the diner's produce order to replace the standard chopped iceberg in the house salad. I can still picture the melamine bowls that came back to the dish station with all of the red lettuces thrown aside. "Why do you have to be so *groovy*?" my dad would ask. "There's a good living to be made here!" I did as any normal teenager would: disregarded everything my parents said because I knew better.

Living in a small town in Maine didn't exactly promise enormous possibilities. During my twenties, I bounced from job to job, waiting tables and bartending, each gig ultimately leaving me feeling empty and lacking purpose.

I tried conjuring up different entrepreneurial ideas. I baked and delivered treats to people's homes. I took familiar family recipes and made them my own, elevating my grandmother's soft molasses cookies with a handful of candied ginger, or using beets in place of carrots in my mother's carrot cake recipe, topping it with a soft, sweet, and tangy goat cheese frosting. This led to a catering job where I taught myself how to make wedding cakes. I fell in love with the process of creating a piece of edible art, soaking layer upon layer of spongy vanilla cake in sweet basil syrup, stacking them with tart lemon curd, meticulously slathering the whole thing with a fluffy buttercream, and dotting it with soft pink peonies. My heart began to sing.

Deep into my twenties, the dream of a formal culinary education burned inside me but was further than distant. I was married and home raising my young son. I didn't have the option to run back to college, and anyhow, I was way past the appropriate age where Mom and Dad would pick up the tuition bill. Instead I found my own way. Working at a local kitchen-supply store, I slowly built a collection of culinary equipment to play with by day and amassed a library of cookbooks to read by night. I picked up more catering gigs to learn new skills and keep on my toes. My mind was constantly churning with what I would do next, how I'd put all this stuff into practice.

And then, one cold and snowy December eve, I opened my apartment door to twenty-four strangers to host the first of a long series of "secret suppers"— and the Lost Kitchen was born. Saturday nights, the light at the bottom of my apartment stoop would flick on and the private door would open, letting in a flood of friends, strangers, and curious food lovers, wine bottles in hand along with a donation to help pay for the cost of the evening. Word spread quickly. People whispered of a new chef, a hidden venue with a blackboard scribbled with the night's menu. The suppers became popular with both locals and out-of-towners. It was there, at the four-burner electric stove in my tiny apartment, that I began to hone my visions of food, inspired by my Maine roots. I infused simple syrup with rosemary and combined it with apple cider and apple brandy to make smooth sorbets. I brined baby chickens with juniper and bay leaves, roasted them in hot skillets with good salty butter and lemon, and served them atop beds of spicy arugula. I roasted beets and pureed them with dill and buttermilk to create cold summer soups that I garnished with borage blossoms and olive oil. I perfected pastry dough and filled the tender crusts with any and every seasonal fruit or berry I could get my hands on.

After a year of rogue suppers, I finally found the courage to open a formal restaurant. I raised the funds from family and friends who believed in my ability and drive. Months later, the Lost Kitchen officially took shape in the commercial space below my apartment. It was beyond my wildest dreams. I had found my footing and made a name, established my place in this world. One evening, at the peak of service, Polly Shyka walked in. She and her husband own Villageside Farm in Freedom. She told me that her father-in-law was spearheading an effort to revive the old mill in town and was toying with the idea of including space for a restaurant. She asked if maybe I'd come check out the space. Who knows, maybe I could even open another spot there. I quickly dismissed the idea—I was working twenty-hour days just to stay afloat.

But life is unpredictable. In May of 2013, the Lost Kitchen took on a new meaning for me: I literally lost the kitchen in the messy end of my marriage. One simple change of the locks and the restaurant of my dreams was gone—along with everything inside. Every skillet, whisk, table, chair, fork and spoon, even my grandmother's dishes. Everything I had worked so hard for and put so much love into. It knocked me on my knees.

So I did the only thing I knew how to do: I kept going. I realized that the heart of my cooking is not defined by the walls of any building, that the Lost Kitchen is defined by my heart, my soul, and my hands. I would rebuild.

Polly's words about the mill echoed in my mind, but the possibility seemed distant and abstract. I needed something real, and real soon—especially if I was going to find work during the rapidly approaching busy summer season. And as is typical for me, change happened in atypical fashion. The ad read:

> FOR SALE: 1965 AIRSTREAM TRADEWIND
> PRICE: BEST OFFER
> LOCATION: BAT CAVE, NC

There was only one thing to do . . . "To the Bat Cave!"

I spent a month gutting the twenty-foot vintage trailer with a sledgehammer (talk about aggression-release!) and my bare hands. I outfitted it with a galley kitchen, collected mismatched dishes and flatware from tag sales, built farmhouse tables from old barn board and cast-iron pipe, and learned how to hitch up and tow a trailer solo. I also went back to my

roots—back to the e-mail list from my supper club. I reached out to all those strangers-turned-friends, a total of five hundred people who would travel to the ends of the earth to eat my food.

The Airstream and I traveled the state, hosting elaborate dinners of farmed and foraged Maine fare in fields, orchards, barns, and greenhouses. I collected wild mustard greens and sea beans to add zing and crunch to lobster salads.

I gathered tiny berries to fill ginger scones and topped them with dollops of fresh whipped cream for summer shortcakes. I filled galvanized buckets with wild rose hips and then pickled them to garnish martinis. I slaughtered dozens of chickens and ducks, using every bit of them—grilling the tender meats over open fires, preparing confit with tougher parts to serve over a bed of lentils with herbs and fried potatoes, making pâtés with sautéed apples and brandy, and simmering flavorful stocks with the carcasses and gizzards for silky root vegetable soups.

As inspiring and fulfilling as this was, I longed for a place where I could put down roots again, a little hole in the world that I could swab, scrub, and paint into new life. I would adorn the tables with handmade runners and arrange them with my vintage plate treasures, along with antique bone dishes filled with olives, old glass milk bottles as water pitchers, and flea market goblets arranged with tulips and pussy willows. It would be simple and elegant, personal and intimate—a place where friends, family, and neighbors would feel at home. Not just at home, but at *my* home. That's when I remembered Polly's visit. I assumed someone else had already filled the empty spot at the mill but decided to check it out anyway.

On my way to Girl Scout meetings as a kid, I used to pass the 1834 gristmill, wilting by the side of Freedom Falls, given life only by the ghosts of the men who had worked there lifetimes ago and the teenagers who assembled there with cans of spray paint. It had once served as the backbone of the farming community but, left to time and the elements, threatened to crumble into the stream below. It looked about as dilapidated as I felt inside.

Now it too had gone through its own transformation. A group of historians, architects, and tradesmen (coordinated by Tony and Sally Grassi, Polly's in-laws) decided that poor mill should be destined for more than kindling. So they came together to bring it back to life—and were still looking for a tenant. When I walked into the empty space, floor covered in sawdust, I knew this would be next. I pitched them my idea, and, despite the fact that my life was in worse shape than the mill, they listened. They paused. "We believe in second chances," they said.

Now the mill stands strong and proud, part of the National Historic Register. It serves as a symbol of old ways found relevant once again. And at its heart is my restaurant, the Lost Kitchen, finally found, in Freedom.

# WELCOME TO MAINE

One of the biggest reasons I love Maine is that it possesses four distinct seasons, defined by their climate, ingredient, and landscape changes. Spring air is filled with the sweet smell of flowers emerging from the still frigid ground, forsythia bushes bursting with golden color, and rhubarb, chives, and asparagus pushing their way upward toward the sunlight. By summer, the fields are tall with green grass and meadow flowers, tomatoes boast ripe perfection, and a dip in the frigid Atlantic waters offers a much-needed respite from the heat. When fall rolls around, brilliant hues of crimson and amber adorn the trees, apples have never tasted so sweet, and I lust after the smell of a roast in the oven— with pie close behind. Soon the first ruthless frost of the season will arrive, with snowstorms to follow in the weeks to come. Roasted root vegetables and pickles and preserves from the summer nourish us as I swathe myself in flannel and wool, along with the dreams of the much-anticipated scallop and shrimp seasons and the bounty of spring once more.

But perhaps what I love most about Maine is that cooking here is so simple. It's not about enormous shopping lists and intricate techniques. Not in the slightest. It's about using what's around and making it taste like the best version of itself. While I've paired many of the dishes here with sides, salads, purees, and the like, these are merely suggestions. In my kitchen—both at home and in the restaurant—I'm cooking whichever protein has shown up at my back door or I've thawed from the freezer and playing matchmaker with whatever else has been farmed or foraged that day. I urge you to mix and match as you please.

Also, some of the ingredients called for in these recipes won't look familiar. And you won't find them at Shop 'n' Save. Not to worry: I've included more commonly found substitutions. But in any case where you don't have *exactly* the constituents I've named, go forth and experiment. Learn to trust your instincts, discover through play, and if all else fails, remember that there are few ails that butter and salt can't cure.

## A NOTE ON INGREDIENTS

Every ingredient called for in these recipes should be the best possible version of itself that you can find. Get to know the people who are the caretakers of your food. Your trust that they're getting you the freshest ingredients possible and their pride in giving you top quality is what makes your food more than food; it's what makes a community.

That said, I highly encourage you to always have on hand a few key ingredients:

**Kosher salt:** This is your all-purpose seasoning. Use it for brining, curing, making confit, and adding flavor.

**Maldon salt:** A delicate, flaky sea salt that's perfect for sprinkling on a dish before serving for both seasoning and texture.

**Freshly ground or cracked black pepper:** From a peppermill or grinder, not preground in a bottle. End of story.

**Kalamata olive oil:** I use this as my all-purpose oil, from searing to finishing. It has a softer, fruitier flavor than extra-virgin olive oil, so it adds to other ingredients instead of trying to be a star on its own.

**Unsalted butter:** Buy unsalted so you can control the seasoning. I go for something local or for really good European butter. Don't buy the cheapest option.

**Seasoned rice wine vinegar:** The secret ingredient for my Macerated Shallot Vinaigrette (page 30), it has the perfect balance of salt, sugar, and delicious acidity.

**Shallots:** For their nuanced flavor, which is distinct from that of onions, and also for Macerated Shallot Vinaigrette (page 30).

## TOOLS TO LIVE BY

I don't have a kitchen full of fancy gadgets, just a few stand-bys. Don't get too caught up with buying expensive cooking implements; my golden rule is that if a tool feels good to hold and use, then you'll feel in control in the kitchen.

**Cast-iron skillets in a multitude of sizes:** These are the timeless workhorses of the kitchen. They're sturdy and all-purpose and can handle a good banging-around, and, with the right care (see opposite), they'll last forever. Plus the heavy bottom means you can get a good sear on just about anything. Collect them as you can.

**Fine-mesh sieve:** Helps make whatever I'm cooking that much more elegant—silkier soups, purees, sorbets, ice creams, custards.

**Fish spatula:** I use this as my all-purpose spatula. I highly recommend splurging on a nice Swiss-made, wood-handled version.

**Knives (start/continue a collection):** They don't have to be fancy. If they're sharp and comfortable to wield, you can use them to do just about anything. Buy a knife sharpener, too.

**Tongs:** Another case where the Swiss know how to do it right.

**Pruning shears and hand saw:** To keep in the car for foraging and for gathering arrangements.

**A good apron:** Keep clean, feel good.

## Cast Iron Is Crucial

Nothing brings me greater joy than a fried egg that doesn't stick to the pan—which is achievable with a well-cared-for cast-iron skillet. The Lodge brand of cast-iron pans is perfectly wonderful, accessibly priced, and still made in the USA. You can also seek out really good vintage cast iron, made before many American iron producers died out—some victims of the Great Depression, some because they turned their focus to military defense for war, and others when cast iron became unpopular in the 1960s and '70s and aluminum and coated pans became trendy. Scour flea markets and auctions (online too) to collect good vintage cast iron when you can.

Look for these favorite vintage American brands:

| | |
|---|---|
| FAVORITE PIQUA | VICTOR |
| GRISWOLD | WAGNER |
| MOUNTAIN IRON | WAPAK |

You'll find the brand name imprinted on the bottom of the skillet.

## Cast-Iron Care

When you first bring your pot home, you'll want to season it to keep food from sticking to the surface. Well-maintained cast iron is better than any nonstick. Love your pan, treat it well, and it will love you in return.

Here's how to season it:

- Preheat your oven to 250°F.

- Set your pan over high heat until hot, then rub the surface with shortening using a paper towel. (I say shortening, e.g., Crisco, because you want a grease with a high smoke point; otherwise you run the risk of having oil go rancid in your skillet. You could also use coconut, vegetable, or olive oil, but only if you're going to wash and season the pan frequently.)

- Put the pan upside down on a rimmed baking sheet and heat in the oven for an hour.

- Turn the oven off and let the pan sit in the oven overnight. Wipe out any excess shortening and it'll be good as new!

Going forward:

- Never use soap and abrasive sponges. If your pot needs a good scrub, use kosher salt, warm water, and a pot scraper. It should go without saying but never put cast iron through the dishwasher.

- After cleaning, dry the pan well over a low burner. It will rust if water is left in the pan.

- Reseason the pan using the steps outlined above whenever you feel like your pan is not performing at its best.

- Some of the recipes here call to cook and serve in the skillet. When I say serve, I mean serve that moment or that day. Don't keep food overnight in the skillet, as it will take on the metallic taste of the pan.

# SPRING

---

## SHOWERS, BUDS & BLOSSOMS

The seemingly everlasting winter has held its grasp far too long. Cabin fever lingers, and we find ourselves bursting with a craving for green grass, budding blossoms, chirping birds, lingering daylight, and the opportunity to shed the layers of clothes we've been trudging around in for months now.

And then, finally, spring arrives. As if it has been sleeping for months, the earth begins to awaken. To me, there is nothing more exciting than the moment the first bit of green, that long-lost and forgotten hue, emerges from the thawing ground. The moment you can throw open the windows and inhale the first breezes that soften the bracing winter air. The moment the stillness comes alive with birdsong and buzzing and a constant trickle from the thaw—when the sweet scents of daffodils and forsythia awaken our senses, fiddleheads make their way through the soil, ramps spread wild over the forest ground, stalks of rhubarb gain height, and spring parsnips (wintered over, now sweet) are finally ready to be pried from the thawing ground. New life, new hope, and new dreams emerge with this season that I wait for most impatiently, the season of new beginnings.

# FIRSTS

Bites to Share on a Balmy Day
    *Radishes & Butter*
    *Quail Eggs & Celery Salt*
Fried Chive Blossoms
Periwinkles in a Skillet with Garlic & Parsley
Spring Bread Salad with Asparagus, Radishes, Peas & Mint
Razor Clam Ceviche with From-Scratch Saltines
Fried Smelts with Caper Mayo, Lemon & Dill
Spinach Salad with Warm Bacon Vinaigrette & Poached Egg

# MAINS

Ramp & Fiddlehead Fried Rice
Whole-Roasted Trout with Parsnip & Herb Hash
Applewood-Grilled Spring Chicken
Maine Shrimp Roll
Shrimp Stew with Toasted Fennel, Lemon & Chives
Wood-Smoked Leg of Lamb with Garlic Scape & Mint Pesto

# SWEETS

Rhubarb Spoon Cake
Chamomile Crème Brûlée
Graham Cracker Pie
Parsnip Needhams
Sorbets for All Seasons
    *Spring: Rhubarb Elderflower Sorbet*
    *Summer: Blueberry-Sweet Tea Sorbet*
    *Fall: Apple Cider & Rosemary Sorbet*
    *Winter: Clemen-Thyme Sorbet*
Sweet Parsnip Cake with Hazelnuts & Mascarpone
Maple & Candied Walnut Ice Cream Sundae

# Bites to Share on a Balmy Day

RADISHES & BUTTER

QUAIL EGGS & CELERY SALT

I like giving my guests something to do—whether it's peel, shuck, dip, or nibble—while I finish getting dinner on the table. Hard-boiled quail eggs (boil them for 5 minutes before chilling in ice water until cold), served with celery salt for sprinkling on top, make for a fun little project, while radishes and butter are a classic pairing that never goes out of style. To see the radishes coming up—they're usually the first growing thing we pull from the soil—is a very exciting herald of warmer weather to come. Because it's such a simple dish, now is the time to find the freshest vegetables possible and to splurge on really good butter.

**Before the grass,** even before the asparagus, there are chives. I get so excited when their little sprouts start poking out of the dirt—at last I can start eating something green after the long winter. So I put them on everything and use the entire herb, including the blossoms that sprout when they've bolted. I usually sprinkle the lovely purple pompoms over dishes. But in this recipe, inspired by my fond memories of the fried onions and doughboys my dad would sell at summer fairs and carnivals, I fry them up whole—like little fluffy blooming onions—making for a great appetizer.

SERVES 4

Vegetable oil, for frying

1 cup all-purpose flour

½ teaspoon table salt

1½ cups sparkling water, or more if needed

24 chive blossoms

Maldon salt

Lemon Chive Mayo (page 37)

# Fried Chive Blossoms

Heat oil in a deep fryer to 375°F or, alternatively, heat 2 inches of oil in a heavy-bottomed pan to the same temperature. (You can test if the oil is ready by dropping a small blob of batter into it; the batter should bubble and brown within 30 to 40 seconds.)

Meanwhile, combine the flour and table salt. Slowly whisk in the sparkling water and mix until smooth—it should be the consistency of a loose pancake batter. If it seems too thick, add a bit more sparkling water.

Working in batches, dip the chive blossoms in the batter until well coated, then drop them into the hot oil. Fry until golden brown, turning occasionally, 1 to 2 minutes.

Transfer the blossoms to paper towels to soak up any excess oil and sprinkle them with Maldon salt. Serve immediately with the mayo for dipping.

As a kid I was always playing with these little snails on the beach—picking them out of tide pools, poking at them so they'd retract back into their shells, and throwing them at my sister. Even though they're everywhere—and completely free for the scavenging—it wasn't until I opened a restaurant that I actually started cooking them. I like to think of this dish as escargots from Maine, because I cook the periwinkles with the traditional French combination of butter, garlic, and parsley in a small cast-iron skillet and then send them out with a needle and thimble to help diners extract the meat from the shells.

SERVES 2

# Periwinkles in a Skillet
## WITH GARLIC & PARSLEY

¼ cup dry white wine

1 large garlic clove, finely chopped

1 cup periwinkles, rinsed under cold water

4 tablespoons (½ stick) unsalted butter

1 tablespoon chopped fresh flat-leaf parsley

Set a small skillet, preferably cast iron, over medium-high heat and pour in the wine. When it comes to a boil, add the garlic and periwinkles and cover the pan. Cook for 4 minutes, then add the butter and continue to cook, uncovered, until the butter is completely melted, just a minute or so.

Remove from the heat, add the parsley, and toss to combine. Serve straight from the skillet.

**Whether for breakfast, lunch, or dinner,** one of my top five things to eat is warm toasted bread soaked through with vinaigrette. And I feel a little bit better about it when I throw in some crunchy greens—or asparagus, radishes, and peas, when the farm stands are brimming over with them this time of year. Seek out a good white bread like a country bâtard or other crusty sourdough loaf—something made with a good, long ferment that gives it a rich, sour flavor.

**SERVES 6**

# Spring Bread Salad
## WITH ASPARAGUS, RADISHES, PEAS & MINT

Preheat the oven to 425°F.

Cut the asparagus into 2-inch pieces, discarding the tough ends. Arrange the pieces in a single layer on a baking sheet, drizzle with 1 tablespoon of the olive oil, and season with salt and pepper. Give the pan a shake to coat the asparagus. Roast until the pieces are tender but still a bit crunchy, about 5 minutes. Set aside to cool to room temperature.

Combine the asparagus, peas, and radishes in a medium bowl.

Heat a medium skillet, preferably cast iron, over medium-high heat, then pour in the remaining 2 tablespoons olive oil. When the oil shimmers, add the bread and cook, turning partway through, until browned, about 4 minutes. Add to the vegetable mixture.

Sprinkle in the mint, pea tendrils, and vinaigrette and toss to dress. Season with more salt and pepper if desired and garnish with a flurry of chives, snipped with kitchen shears.

1 pound asparagus

3 tablespoons olive oil

Salt and pepper

1 cup shelled fresh peas, blanched (see page 31)

2 bunches of mixed radishes, such as French breakfast and any other beautiful radishes that catch your eye, halved

3 cups torn bread

2 tablespoons chopped fresh mint

2 cups pea tendrils or pea shoots

3 tablespoons Macerated Shallot Vinaigrette (page 30)

Fresh chives

# MACERATED SHALLOT VINAIGRETTE

Oh, the beauty of shallots and vinegar. I actually discovered this now kitchen staple of mine by accident when I made a fresh shallot vinaigrette, left things sitting a little longer than usual, and came back to find how nice and sweet the shallots had become. It turns out that letting them macerate in vinegar for at least twenty minutes completely softens their aggressive onion flavor. In fact, it evolves into a completely different flavor altogether—bright and briny, but savory too. I mix the shallots with olive oil and black pepper to make a vinaigrette, which I call my secret sauce because just a spoonful enhances and brightens everything it touches, adding a little acid and brightness wherever needed. Toss lettuces with just enough to make them glisten. Combine with thinly sliced beets, carrots, or cabbage for a slaw. Drizzle over thinly sliced raw scallops for a crudo.

MAKES ABOUT ½ CUP

1 shallot, finely diced

2 tablespoons seasoned rice wine vinegar, or enough to just cover the shallots

¼ cup olive oil

A couple twists of pepper

Combine the shallots and rice vinegar and allow to macerate for at least 20 minutes or up to overnight. Whisk in the olive oil and pepper. You could store this in your fridge for up to a week, but you'll get the freshest, brightest flavor if you use it within 24 hours.

## The Art of the Flea Market

Come warm weather, the treasures worth hunting for aren't necessarily poking out of the ground. After Memorial Day, auctions and tag sales and flea markets are in full swing, promising pearls of the dusty, rusty, and slightly worn variety—plus plenty of bad coffee, good egg sandwiches, and great people watching. For anyone with the inclination, patience, and backbone to dicker, these markets are the perfect way to create a special collection in your home and on your table.

I've always had a soft spot for special hand-me-downs. There's nothing like the thrill of finding real silver utensils for $1 a piece (or only 50 cents if you're willing to polish it yourself!), vintage Limoges porcelain, or serving platters of all shapes and sizes. Every piece has a story and was at one time beloved by someone, a narrative that keeps unfolding once you've brought the piece home with you. I particularly love estate sales, or what are sometimes called "country auctions." You can go online earlier in the week to see what'll be up for grabs. Always on my hunt-for list: silverware, serving pieces, vintage mirrors, lamps, plates (especially those that match patterns I already have), and chairs. Just remember to bring plenty of cash—many vendors offer a 10 percent discount for not using a credit card, but you have to ask.

## Blanching Vegetables

Blanching is one of those fancy-sounding techniques that is really quite simple. You drop vegetables into a pot of rapidly boiling water, remove them just as they turn vibrantly colored and toothsome, then immediately chill them in ice water—gently cooking them but preserving their just-picked freshness.

Here's the basic method:

Bring a large pot of water to a boil and add a fistful of salt. The water should taste salty. Toss in the vegetables in small batches to make sure they have room to bob about and the water stays at a rolling boil. Let them cook for 20 to 30 seconds, then test to see if they're tender; it will happen quickly. Once they're ready, scoop them out with a slotted spoon and dunk them in an ice bath (a large bowl filled with ice water). Once cool, drain well.

I'm pretty sure my obsession with clam necks—which are chewier than the bellies, almost more scallop than oyster—comes from the dip my Gram used to make. It was pretty much just canned clams and mayonnaise, but it was a classic nonetheless, ranking up there with shrimp and lobster salad.

When I found a good source for razor clams, I immediately thought of Gram's beloved dip because, unlike their steamer cousins with their soft little bellies, these are pretty much all neck, like a clam strip. By swapping out canned clams for just-caught ones, marinating them in lime juice, adding a bed of homemade saltines, and perfuming the whole dish with the first wisps of sprouting baby cilantro, I've taken Gram's dip from potluck staple to something as fresh as sea air.

If you'll be shucking the clams yourself, steam them for a few seconds to make the shells easier to open. And if you can't find razor clams, you could substitute scallops or shrimp.

SERVES 6

# Razor Clam Ceviche
## WITH FROM-SCRATCH SALTINES

2 pounds razor clams, shucked (have your fishmonger do this if you are squeamish, but ask him to reserve the shells)

1 tablespoon finely chopped shallot

2 teaspoons seasoned rice wine vinegar

Juice of 2 limes

1 tablespoon olive oil

½ jalapeño, seeded and thinly sliced

1 tablespoon chopped fresh cilantro

½ cup pea tendrils or pea shoots

Maldon salt

Violets, for garnish (optional)

From-Scratch Saltines (page 34)

Wash the reserved clam shells for serving and set aside.

Slice the clam meat into ¼-inch slices and put in a medium bowl. Add the shallot, vinegar, and lime juice and stir to incorporate. Cover the bowl with plastic wrap or a clean towel and put in the refrigerator to cure for 30 minutes.

Add the olive oil, jalapeño, cilantro, and pea tendrils to the clams and toss to combine.

Put a small dollop of the clam mixture in each shell and sprinkle with Maldon salt and violet petals, if using. Alternatively, mound the ceviche in a pretty bowl. Serve with the saltines.

**Buying Razor Clams**

Make sure your clams are alive when you buy them; they should retract into their shells when you touch them. Store them so they can still breathe—covered with a clean cloth, not sealed in a plastic bag—in the refrigerator. Give them a good rinse under cold water before using them.

# FROM-SCRATCH SALTINES

Few homes in New England are without a box of saltines in the pantry. Whether you crumble them over chowder, dip them into shrimp salad, or mound them under scoops of just-melting vanilla ice cream—à la my grandmother—the effort to make these from scratch will pay big dividends.

Preheat the oven to 375°F. Line a baking sheet with parchment paper.

In a large bowl, combine the flour and baking powder. Work in the coconut oil with a pastry blender until well incorporated. Stir in the milk and form the dough into a ball.

Roll out the dough on a floured surface to ⅛ inch thick. Brush the dough with the butter, then cut it into 1½-inch squares. Transfer to the baking sheet, spacing the squares at least ½ inch apart. Sprinkle with Maldon salt. Bake until the edges begin to brown slightly, 12 to 15 minutes.

Use a spatula to transfer the crackers to a wire rack and let cool. The crackers will keep in a sealed container at room temperature for up to 1 week.

MAKES ABOUT
36 CRACKERS

4 cups all-purpose flour, plus more for rolling the dough

1 teaspoon baking powder

¾ cup coconut oil

1¼ cups whole milk

4 tablespoons (½ stick) unsalted butter, melted

Maldon salt

### A Note on Crackers

A pasta roller can double as an amazing device for consistently thin crackers. Consider the investment!

**I find that you're either a smelt enthusiast or you're not.** The people who love them all but freak out when they see them on the menu come late winter and early spring: "The smelts are running!"

Fried smelts are basically like little fish French fries. You can buy the fish from the fishmonger all ready to go, gutted and headless (the spine bones are left in, but they're delicate enough that they're meant to be eaten); then you don't have to do anything but fry them up and serve them with lemon wedges and caper mayonnaise, otherwise known as do-it-yourself tartar sauce. Ideally you'll find the little guys, no longer than four inches.

**SERVES 4**

# Fried Smelts
## WITH CAPER MAYO, LEMON & DILL

Vegetable oil, for frying

1 cup all-purpose flour

Salt

1 (12-ounce) bottle of white ale, such as Allagash (plus more to drink while cooking)

1 pound smelts

Dill fronds, snipped

Caper Mayo (opposite)

Cornichons

Lemon wedges

Heat the oil in a deep fryer to 375°F or, alternatively, heat 2 inches of oil in a heavy-bottomed pan to the same temperature. (You can test if the oil is ready by dropping a small blob of batter into it; the batter should bubble and then brown within 30 to 40 seconds.)

Make a batter by combining the flour and ½ teaspoon salt in a medium bowl. Slowly whisk in the beer and continue whisking until smooth. The batter should be thick enough to coat the back of a spoon.

Drag each smelt through the batter and drop into the oil, frying about 4 at a time (overcrowding the fryer will lower the oil temperature and make for a soggy coating). Fry until golden brown, turning if necessary to brown both sides, 3 to 4 minutes. Blot on brown paper bags or paper towels, sprinkle with salt and dill fronds, and serve immediately with caper mayo, cornichons, and lemon wedges.

# HOMEMADE MAYO

Some people might call this "aioli," but here in Maine it's just mayonnaise. A homemade version is a staple in my mind, serving as the foundation for about a million things in the kitchen. Add some buttermilk and you have a creamy dressing. Throw in some rosemary and you have a delicious sauce for frites. Stir in curry powder or citrus zest and you've made an amazing dip for calamari. It keeps in the fridge for up to a week, but it never lasts that long!

Making mayonnaise is very simple. A guy named Ken used to work for me, and he'd come in every day for his shift and make a big batch of our mayonnaise by hand. He'd be whisking for twenty minutes. Come summer, Ken left the restaurant to go back to work on his farm. We were beside ourselves—who was going to make the mayonnaise?! Finally, someone piped up and said, "Why don't we just use the hand mixer?" We've been doing it that way ever since (though using a food processor is even easier).

The basic ratio for mayonnaise is usually one egg yolk to every cup of oil. But as extra insurance against breaking, I use two yolks. As for oil, I recommend using a neutral-tasting oil (like vegetable), though if you really love olive oil and want that flavor to shine through, go for it.

Use a handheld mixer or a whisk to combine the yolks and garlic in a large bowl. Continue mixing as you start to incorporate the oil very slowly, almost drop by drop. As extra insurance against breaking, add oil only about every other second for about 60 seconds, mixing all the while. Then once it begins to get thick and fluffy, add the oil in a steadier stream. Continue mixing until all the oil has emulsified into the egg mixture. Add the lemon juice and season with salt to taste. You can also thin out the mayo with a little water, so feel free to adjust the consistency to your liking.

If your mayo starts to look thin and greasy instead of fluffy and creamy, don't throw it away! Simply set aside what you've done and start over. Then, once you've gotten the new mixture to emulsify, whisk in the old batch. Then add the lemon juice and season to taste.

MAKES 1½ CUPS

2 large egg yolks

½ garlic clove, minced or grated

1 cup vegetable oil

½ teaspoon fresh lemon juice

Salt

## Lemon Chive Mayo

Mix the juice of ½ lemon into the mayo and sprinkle with chopped chives before serving.

## Caper Mayo

Mix 2 to 3 tablespoons chopped drained brined capers into the mayo.

## Horseradish Mayo

Mix 1 tablespoon prepared horseradish into the mayo.

## Tartar Sauce

Add ⅓ cup chopped pickles to the mayo. I like bread-and-butter for a sweet, old-fashioned taste, but any pickle will do.

**My mom made this salad** whenever she didn't have time to make anything else. There were always eggs and bacon on hand, plus a handful of spinach or whatever greens were still looking good in the garden or crisper, and boom—something's on the table. It's the perfect warm salad for a cold day.

**SERVES 4**

# Spinach Salad
## WITH WARM BACON VINAIGRETTE & POACHED EGG

Start by preparing the vinaigrette. In a small saucepan, let the shallots macerate in the vinegar for 20 minutes or until softened. Add the olive oil and bacon and warm slowly over low heat.

Meanwhile, make the croutons. Drizzle just enough oil to coat the bottom of a large skillet, preferably cast iron, and heat over medium-high heat. Add the bread cubes and toast, continually shaking the pan, until golden on all sides, about 4 minutes.

Put the spinach in a large bowl and toss with the warm croutons and vinaigrette. Don't use all the dressing at first, only enough to coat the spinach. Use your hands to mix, so you can feel how well the salad is dressed. Then add more vinaigrette as needed. Use your instincts!

Divide the salad among 4 plates. Gently ladle an egg over the top of each salad. Finish with a sprinkle of salt and a twist of fresh pepper.

1 small shallot, sliced into thin rings

2 tablespoons seasoned rice wine vinegar

¼ cup olive oil, plus more for the pan

6 slices of bacon, cooked and roughly chopped

4 slices of crusty bread, cut into 1-inch cubes

4 good handfuls (or 2 cups packed) of fresh spinach

4 large eggs, poached (see below)

Salt and pepper

**Poaching Eggs**

I use a 12-inch skillet for 4 eggs, 8-inch for 2. Fill a skillet with an inch or two of water and bring to a boil over high heat. Meanwhile, crack the eggs individually into small bowls so you have a chance to fish out any stray shell bits. Carefully slide the eggs into the water and poach—keeping the water at a boil—until the white is set but the yolk is still soft, 3 to 4 minutes. Remove the eggs from the pan with a slotted spoon and dab the bottom of the spoon on a paper towel to absorb excess water.

# Ramp & Fiddlehead Fried Rice

**My friend Ashley lives on an amazing property** that seems to stretch on forever, dotted with rolling hills, gurgling streams, and a secret pond with not a single person or thing to share it. It's heaven.

One evening last spring, we set out in the full-moon light with a basket, a bottle of Prosecco, and our dogs to see what we could forage for dinner. As luck would have it, we hit the springtime jackpot: fiddleheads and ramps.

Fiddleheads are the very beginnings of ferns that are still coiled, the most coveted of which come from the ostrich fern. When cooked properly, they still have a little crunch—like perfectly cooked asparagus (which make a fine substitute in a pinch)—and taste the way fresh ferns smell: grassy and earthy and herbaceous. You need to catch them at the exact right time since the tighter their spirals, the better. Once they start to unfurl, they get bitter.

Ramps are wild onions. They look a little like scallions (which, again, make a fine alternative) with their white bulbs and green shoots, but they have a woodsier taste and are even spicier. You can find them growing by streams and dig them out with a small garden tool, or you could just go to a farmer's market, where they're usually abundant, though for only a month each spring.

All we had to do next was forage a bouquet for the table, sauté up our haul, pair it with simple pantry staples—eggs and rice—and call it a meal.

**SERVES 4**

2 cups rice, ideally black, but brown will work too

Salt and pepper

4 tablespoons olive oil, plus more for drizzling

6 ramps or scallions, sliced—greens, bulbs, and all

¾ pound fiddleheads or asparagus (cut into 1½-inch pieces), blanched (see page 31)

3 tablespoons seasoned rice wine vinegar, plus more for drizzling

4 large eggs, fried or poached (page 38)

Microgreens, for garnish (optional)

**Note:**

This dish also makes a lovely side dish if you omit the egg. It pairs particularly nicely with Applewood-Grilled Spring Chicken (page 49).

First, cook the rice. There are very few small appliances that I love, but my rice cooker is one of them—perfect rice every time! Use yours and follow the manufacturer's directions. If you don't have one, bring the rice, 3½ cups water, and ½ teaspoon salt to a boil in a heavy-bottomed saucepan, uncovered, over medium-high heat. Cover, reduce the heat to low, and simmer until the rice is tender and most of the water has been absorbed, about 35 minutes. With either method, rinse the cooked rice with cold water, drain well, and spread over a baking sheet. Chill in the refrigerator for a few hours or overnight (this will help it get nice and crispy when you fry it).

Heat 2 tablespoons of the olive oil in a large skillet, preferably cast iron, over medium-high heat. Add the ramps and fiddleheads, ½ teaspoon salt, and a few twists of fresh pepper. Sauté until the greens have wilted and the whites have just begun to brown, about 2 minutes.

Raise the heat to high and add the remaining 2 tablespoons olive oil and the rice. Let it be without stirring for 15 to 20 seconds, then give the pan a good stir or shake. Continue frying the rice, stirring occasionally, until crisp, about 4 minutes. Add the vinegar, give the pan another good stir, and remove from the heat.

Toss the microgreens, if using, with a drizzle of olive oil, a splash of vinegar, and a pinch of salt.

Divide the fried rice among 4 plates, top each plate with a fried egg, and garnish with the greens, if using, and a twist of black pepper.

It makes me really happy when someone orders a roasted whole trout at the restaurant. It means I get to reach down into the bed of ice where the fish are resting, pull one out, and witness almost everyone in the space turn to watch me balance this glossy, iridescent creature on my forearm as I prepare a cast-iron pan for searing. There's no better reminder of where food comes from than looking into its eyes. And, of course, there's something so impressive and gorgeous about serving a fish whole, particularly one that's been stuffed with lemon and herbs.

This dish is amazing when cooked over a wood fire, but if that's not an option, a trusty cast-iron pan and a hot oven will do.

**SERVES 4**

# Whole-Roasted Trout
## WITH PARSNIP & HERB HASH

Preheat the oven to 425°F.

Salt and pepper the trout inside and out and stuff each with 2 lemon slices and some thyme.

Heat a large ovenproof skillet, preferably cast iron, over high heat and pour in the olive oil. Add the fish and cook until the skin turns golden, about 4 minutes. Flip the fish and cook for 1 minute on the stovetop before transferring the pan to the oven. After a minute in the oven, put 1 tablespoon butter on top of each trout, then continue roasting until the fish is just cooked through, 12 to 15 minutes. Serve drizzled with a bit of the pan juices alongside a skillet of the parsnip hash.

4 small trout (around 1 pound each)

Salt and pepper

2 lemons, cut into 4 slices each, ends reserved for juice

1 bunch of fresh thyme

2 tablespoons olive oil

4 tablespoons (½ stick) unsalted butter

Spring-Dug-Parsnip Hash (opposite)

# SPRING-DUG-PARSNIP HASH

Hash was a staple in my family when I was growing up. Especially when we were camping, my dad was always throwing beets, carrots, potatoes—any root vegetables, really—into a cast-iron skillet and cooking them to a lovely char, the wood fire lending another layer of flavor. The vegetables would be caramelized and crispy on the outside yet soft and creamy on the inside. In this version, I pair parsnips with carrots because I love their natural sweetness, but you could easily substitute celery root, sweet potato, beets, turnips, or regular potatoes.

I prefer to leave the skins on the parsnips and carrots. Dice them into ½-inch pieces and blanch (see page 31) until just al dente; start testing for tenderness after 10 minutes. Drain and refrigerate until just cool.

Heat 1 tablespoon of the olive oil in a 10-inch cast-iron pan over low heat. Add the shallots and cook, stirring occasionally, until deeply caramelized, about 20 minutes.

Raise the heat to medium and add the remaining tablespoon olive oil, the butter, and thyme. Stir to melt the butter. Add the parsnips and carrots and stir to coat. Season with 1 teaspoon salt and a couple twists of pepper and continue cooking until the parsnips begin to brown, stirring only occasionally to keep them from burning, 6 to 8 minutes.

Taste and adjust the seasoning if needed. Remove from the heat and stir in the dill and chives. Serve family-style out of the skillet.

SERVES 4

1½ pounds parsnips

½ pound carrots

2 tablespoons olive oil

6 large shallots, sliced

4 tablespoons (½ stick) unsalted butter

2 tablespoons fresh thyme leaves

Salt and pepper

6 sprigs of fresh dill, snipped

2 tablespoons chopped fresh chives

Cooking whole chicken on the grill is particularly well suited for spring chickens (also known as poussins), which are younger and smaller than the 4- to 6-pound roasting birds you see at the store. (Cornish game hens also work well here.) I like to poach my chicken in brine before grilling, so the bird spends just enough time over the fire to crisp up and soak in that smoky flavor—and not dry out. It's also great insurance that your meat is fully cooked.

I prefer applewood here, which lends a hint of sweetness, though you can use all different types of woods for this. My simple rule is: Does it produce food? If it's a tree that yields something edible—like maple, cherry, and apple—then chances are its wood is also going to create something for the greater good of your stomach. While I gather my wood from the trees on my property, you could easily use chips from the store.

**SERVES 6**

# Applewood–Grilled Spring Chicken

2 whole spring chickens (2½ to 3 pounds each)

Basic Brine (page 170)

½ cup maple syrup

8 tablespoons (1 stick) unsalted butter

Apple blossoms, for garnish (optional)

Truss the birds (see page 50) and submerge them in the cool brine and refrigerate overnight.

In a large pot over medium heat, bring the chicken and brine to a slow boil. Reduce the heat and simmer until just cooked through, 15 to 20 minutes. Immediately remove the chicken from the brine and let cool to room temperature.

Prepare the grill as described on page 51 using applewood branches or chips. Once the fire tames and the wood ashes over, rake the hot embers to one side of the grill. You don't want the chicken to burn instead of becoming infused with smoky flavor.

In a small saucepan, combine the maple syrup and butter; stir until the butter is melted and well incorporated.

*(recipe continues)*

Put the birds breast-side down on the cooler side of the grill. Cover the grill and keep the air vents half open. Adjust if needed, closing them more if the fire gets too hot; if you have a probe thermometer, you're aiming for 325°F to 375°F. Once the first side is browned, about 8 minutes, turn the chicken. Using a pastry brush, baste the chicken with the butter mixture frequently, covering the grill in between basting. Continue to rotate and baste the chicken until golden brown, about 15 minutes more. Keep an eye on the chicken, as the fire needs to be tended constantly to avoid getting too hot.

Serve the chickens on a platter garnished with apple blossoms, if desired.

## "No Strings Attached" Trussing

This method is not only easier than using string, but also sort of a necessity for me. I'm often caught without trussing string on hand—and it's an hour round-trip to go out and buy some! It is important to truss, though, as it helps keep the extremities closer to the body, which prevents overcooking.

First, take the wing tips and tuck them behind the body, almost like the chicken has its arms behind its back. Next, go to the bottom of the breastbone where you'll find an extra flap of skin. Make a tiny slit, about ¼ inch long, and pull each drumstick through. Done!

## Playing with Fire:

## PREPARING THE GRILL AND KEEPING THE FIRE GOING

When it comes to grilling, there are two kinds of people: those who have fire in their blood, and those who don't. I'm the latter—it took me a while to figure out how to get a fire started, keep it going, and then use it to cook the perfect piece of meat. I found that it's a lot like sailing: you have to constantly adjust. You don't walk away from a grill; you have to sit with it, stay with it, and play with it. It's different every time you grill, too. So while I can give you the basic steps, you have to feel it out based on your own environment and circumstances. Grilling is definitely an intuitive exercise. As for what kind of grill to use—keep it simple. I'm addicted to my basic, inexpensive Weber.

Here's how I prepare a grill:

- If you have a chimney starter, stuff it with newspaper and coals, light the paper, and let the coals heat up before dumping them into the bottom of the grill. If not, ignite a layer of coals on the bottom of the grill (a little lighter fluid is okay here, a little cheat for getting things going). If you have kindling, throw some of that in there, too.

- If using branches, start layering in some smaller pieces of wood. (If you're using wood chips, soak them in cold water for about 20 minutes.)

- When the fire gets nice and hot, pour or rake the coals down and off to one side. This gives you a cooking area where the heat isn't so intense, so the meat can cook long enough to soak up all that smoky goodness. But if you need a good sear, you can use the side with the coals. Put the grill grate in place and wait for the flames

to die out until they're just smoldering and the coals are covered with white ash.

- If you're using wood chips, drain them and toss a handful on the hot coals.

- Close the oxygen feeds at the top and bottom of the grill most of the way. You need a little air to keep the coals going, but you'll want to play with this as you cook in order to adjust the temperature. The more oxygen that comes in, the hotter the grill. When you want a slow burn, like for lamb, you don't want a lot of oxygen.

- Add the meat and cover the grill.

- If cooking for longer periods of time, add more wood or hot coals to the fire as necessary.

- Use an instant-read thermometer to gauge if your meat is done.

A **shrimp roll**—or crispy, golden shrimp piled high on a buttered, griddled, and tartar sauce–slathered bun—is a classic way to enjoy some of our state's favorite seafood. Serve with lemon wedges, pickles, and chips and call it a day.

SERVES 4

# Maine Shrimp Roll

Butter the cut sides of the rolls and grill, toast, or griddle buttered-side down until golden brown. Slather the inside of each roll with a tablespoon of tartar sauce and line with baby lettuces.

Heat oil in a deep fryer to 375°F or, alternatively, heat 2 inches of oil in a heavy-bottomed pan to the same temperature.

Combine the shrimp and the milk in large bowl. Whisk together the all-purpose and semolina flours in a separate bowl.

Working in batches, drain the shrimp, dredge in the flour mixture until well coated, and then fry until golden brown, about 20 seconds.

Fill the prepared rolls with the hot shrimp and serve immediately.

3 tablespoons unsalted butter, at room temperature

4 hot dog rolls, split

4 tablespoons Tartar Sauce (page 37)

4 small handfuls of baby lettuce

Vegetable oil, for frying

1 pound shelled Maine shrimp

1 cup whole milk

¾ cup all-purpose flour

¾ cup semolina flour

## Maine Shrimp Soup and Sandwich

When it's shrimp season, you're eating shrimp All. The. Time. There are trucks parked everywhere, selling shrimp caught just hours before. Because they're dirt-cheap, you buy pounds and pounds of them, and then you sit at the table for hours peeling them, picking off those delicate iridescent shells. After all that hard work, it's pretty much all you can do but eat shrimp.

If you have the time, get the freshest shrimp you can—meaning whole—and do the work. They're cheaper, fresher, and taste better—and I promise it'll be gratifying when you're done; you'll feel like you accomplished something. Plus, shrimp freeze really well. Just be mindful that Maine shrimp are not like big Gulf shrimp. Everyone knows that shrimp cook fast and you don't want to overcook them. Well, these cook even more quickly because they're a lot smaller. The key is to boil them in salted water for no more than 10 seconds, then transfer them to an ice bath to stop the cooking because otherwise they'll turn to mush.

**Seafood stew was one of the first things** my dad ever let me cook when I was fourteen and just starting to work on the line at the diner. There were three kinds—shrimp, scallop, and lobster—and we'd "make it to order." We'd take a mug, put in a handful of raw seafood, add a heaping spoonful of butter from the brick sitting on the counter, top it off with half-and-half, and then microwave it until it was hot. If Dad was feeling really fancy, we'd sprinkle on some dried parsley and paprika, park a lemon wedge on the rim, and serve a little bag of oyster crackers on the side. People loved it, and he still makes it like that to this day. I'm not one to knock an old standby, but this version offers something a little more elevated. Serve it with From-Scratch Saltines (page 34) if you're feeling ambitious.

SERVES 4

# Shrimp Stew
## WITH TOASTED FENNEL, LEMON & CHIVES

1 tablespoon fennel seed

2 cups heavy cream

2 cups whole milk

4 tablespoons (½ stick) unsalted butter

4 shallots, sliced

2 tablespoons olive oil

Salt and pepper

1 pound shelled Maine shrimp

Grated zest and juice of 1 lemon

2 tablespoons chopped fresh chives

In a small skillet over medium-high heat, toast the fennel seeds, tossing frequently, until they become aromatic, 3 to 4 minutes. Remove from the pan and set aside to cool.

Combine the cream, milk, and butter in a medium saucepan and bring just to a boil over medium heat. Add the fennel seeds, turn off the heat, and cover the pan. Let the seeds steep for 15 to 20 minutes, then strain to remove the seeds.

Meanwhile, heat the shallots in a medium skillet with the olive oil and a pinch each of salt and pepper over low heat until soft and deeply browned, about 20 minutes.

Add the caramelized shallots to the fennel-infused cream and bring to a simmer. Turn off the heat. Add the shrimp and lemon zest and juice. Season with salt and pepper to taste, sprinkle with chives, and serve.

**This is day-off food for me**—I just get my grill going, throw in some wood, and make a nice, slow Sunday dish to have for an early and relaxed dinner. When I was a kid, my mom would make lamb as a special occasion dish and serve it with mint jelly—a classic pairing. This dish calls on those same tried-and-true flavors but takes the whole thing to a more laid-back place.

You don't need some fancy smoker setup; you can do this on your back stoop on your Weber. And if you don't have a grill, you can make this in the oven.

SERVES 6

# Wood-Smoked Leg of Lamb
## WITH GARLIC SCAPE & MINT PESTO

6 garlic cloves, crushed

¾ cup olive oil

Grated zest and juice of 1 lemon

1 bunch of fresh mint, finely chopped

2 teaspoons salt

10 good twists of black pepper

1 semiboneless leg of lamb (3 to 4 pounds)

Garlic Scape & Mint Pesto (opposite)

In a baking dish large enough to hold the lamb, combine the garlic, olive oil, lemon zest and juice, mint, salt, and pepper. Add the lamb, slather with the marinade, cover with plastic wrap, and refrigerate for at least 8 hours or overnight.

**TO GRILL:** Prepare the grill (see page 51). Scrape the coals to one side of the grill and put the lamb on the cooler side. Cover and smoke, checking the lamb frequently and turning to cook all sides until nicely browned. Keep both the heat low and the oxygen intake low. Add additional hot coals and/or wood as needed. The goal is to let the lamb spend a good 45 minutes to an hour on the grill soaking up the smoky flavor, but not burning. The lamb is done when an instant-read thermometer inserted into the meat—in a thick spot that's not right on the bone—reads 145°F.

**TO ROAST IN THE OVEN:** Preheat the oven to 425°F.

Put the lamb in a roasting pan—marinade and all—and cook until an instant-read thermometer reads 145°F, about 1½ hours.

Transfer the cooked meat to a cutting board and let rest for 15 minutes. Slice and serve with the pesto.

# GARLIC SCAPE & MINT PESTO

If left to its own devices, mint will overrun a garden to the point where you have to pull it out by the fistful. To put a bunch of it to good use, substitute it for traditional basil in this refreshing twist on an old standby.

In a food processor, pulse the scapes, mint leaves, pine nuts, and pecorino until well combined. With the machine running, slowly drizzle in the olive oil. Add the lemon zest and juice, pulse, taste, and season with salt and pepper. This is best used the day it's made, but it'll keep in the fridge for up to a week.

1 bunch of garlic scapes (about 1 pound), blanched (see page 31), well drained, and roughly chopped

1 bunch of fresh mint, leaves only

¼ cup pine nuts, toasted

¼ cup grated pecorino

½ cup olive oil

Grated zest and juice of ½ lemon

Salt and pepper

## Garlic Scapes

When these come into season in midsummer, farmers literally show up with them by the trash bagful. They have so many that I'm essentially doing them a favor by taking the scapes off their hands. Luckily, the spicy, garlicky flavor of these shoots is really versatile—you can grill or roast them like asparagus with a drizzle of olive oil, squeeze of lemon, and pinch of salt; chop them up and whip them into softened butter; fry them in a tempura batter and serve with mayo for dipping; or make a simple pesto that is delicious with rich grilled meats.

## Meat Shares and Stocking the Larder

I don't order meat the way most restaurants do. Instead, I usually wait for farmers in the area to give me the heads-up that their animals are going to slaughter. Then I send a cut list—or list of various cuts or preparations I'd like—and store the eventual delivery in my freezer. Most of the folks around here do the same thing for their own homes, but instead of buying a whole animal—which can be expensive and yield too much meat for one family— they participate in what's called an animal share. It's an economical way to source high-quality lamb, beef, pork, or goat from farmers observing the best possible husbandry practices and get exactly what you want how you want it: ground, cured, Frenched; shanks, loins, legs, chops— you name it. That said, it's less a luxury here than a necessity. In rural Maine, there's nothing coming out of the ground come winter, nor are the animals going to slaughter. And I can't exactly go running out to Whole Foods. So protein-wise, I plan ahead in the warmer months and freeze as much meat, fish, and seafood as I can. Investing in a meat share is one great way to fill your larder and give you plenty of options for things to cook during the colder months.

## Spring Cleaning

I found my hand sink under a pile of scrap chicken wire in the back corner of my parents' barn. My mother pulled it out one spring while cleaning and gave it a quick scrub with Bon Ami. "Do you have any interest in this old thing?" she asked. My eyes lit up. This was the sink that was in our farmhouse bathroom during my childhood. I washed my hands in it every day as a little girl. I said my first word standing in front of it, scrubbing up and looking out the window across the pasture toward the pond: "Horsey!"

In short, I love that old cast-iron sink, which now sits in the corner of my kitchen here at TLK as our hand-washing station. Over the past year I've laughed while leaning over it, cried in it, and used it to soothe burns on a busy Saturday night. It leaks constantly and annoyingly has separate hot and cold taps—one side scalding, the other frigid, no in-between. (The trick is to turn both on at once and move your hands quickly back and forth between both sides.) During our initial state health inspection, the inspector looked at it and then me with disapproval, announcing, "This won't work." I encouraged him to reconsider. Because this wasn't just a sink to me; it was a piece of my life. In the end, I was able to keep the sink where it was. Every evening after service I have to turn the water off at the pipe so that it doesn't drip away through the night, racking up the water bill.

In many ways, that sink is a lot like my own home—perfectly imperfect. I cherish the dings and dents, celebrate the worn and torn. So every year come spring, when I throw open the windows and let the fresh air slip into every possible space, I am thankful that it is there to help me with my spring cleaning.

## LAVENDER SINK SCRUB

This gentle, nontoxic cleaner is perfect for giving any sink—or any porcelain, cast-iron, or enamel surface, for that matter—some tender loving care. Sprinkle the cleaner where needed, drizzle a little natural dish soap on top, scrub, and rinse with hot water. Voilà!

**MAKES 2 CUPS**

½ cup dried lavender, finely ground in a spice grinder

1 (14-ounce) box baking soda

In a medium bowl, stir together the lavender and baking soda. Transfer to a sugar shaker for easy application.

## ROSE WATER GLASS CLEANER

Reducing chemicals around my home is important to me. Here is a simple recipe for a nontoxic glass and window cleaner that will spell the end for that ammonia-scented blue bottle lurking in the cabinet under your sink. The vinegar is a powerful cleanser while the rose water provides a welcome fragrance.

**MAKES 1 QUART**

½ cup distilled white vinegar

½ cup rubbing alcohol

2 cups rose water

1 cup water

Combine the ingredients in a clean spray bottle.

I wish I could say this dessert was the product of consideration and foresight, but then it might not have been as delicious. When I had my very own first rhubarb patch, I was excited to harvest it and cook it into a beautiful cake to impress my supper club. But I added too much butter and not enough flour, and I ended up with a pink and white swirly mess. But something really magical had happened—it tasted like gooey vanilla cake with warmed compote mixed in. Now when I serve this (purposefully), I hand out spoons and we all dig in.

SERVES 8

# Rhubarb Spoon Cake

8 tablespoons (1 stick) unsalted butter, melted, plus more for the pan

1 cup all-purpose flour, plus more for the pan

2 teaspoons baking powder

½ cup sugar

½ teaspoon salt

1 large egg

1 teaspoon vanilla extract

½ cup whole milk

¼ cup sour cream

Rhubarb Compote (page 62)

Perfectly Whipped Cream (page 62)

Preheat the oven to 400°F. Coat a 10-inch ovenproof skillet, preferably cast iron, with butter and flour, shaking out any excess flour.

In a medium bowl, combine the flour, baking powder, sugar, and salt. In a large bowl, whisk together the egg, vanilla, milk, sour cream, and melted butter. Gently stir the wet ingredients into the dry until just incorporated.

Pour about two-thirds of the compote into the greased skillet and spread evenly. Pour the cake batter over it, spread evenly, then dollop the remaining compote over the top. Use a butter knife to swirl together the batter and compote.

Bake until a cake tester or knife inserted in the middle of the cake comes out clean, about 25 minutes. I like to serve this warm, directly from the skillet, with a big spoon and a bowl of whipped cream to dollop on top.

## RHUBARB COMPOTE

In a medium heavy-bottomed saucepan, combine the rhubarb, sugar, lemon zest, lemon juice, and cornstarch. Bring to a simmer over medium heat, stirring constantly until the rhubarb becomes tender and sauce-like, about 5 minutes. Remove from the heat and allow to cool to room temperature. This will keep in the fridge for up to a week.

MAKES ABOUT 3 CUPS

3 cups chopped rhubarb (1-inch pieces)

⅔ cup sugar

1 teaspoon grated lemon zest

2 teaspoons fresh lemon juice

2 teaspoons cornstarch

## PERFECTLY WHIPPED CREAM

We keep things pretty simple at the restaurant. Even our job interviews are basic—I don't care if someone comes in with no experience; I'm really just feeling out their personality. But if I ever had to choose between two people whom I liked equally, I'd ask them to do two things: plate a salad and make whipped cream.

Salads need to look and feel like the leaves floated down from the heavens, high and tight. Whipped cream should be balanced with just a little sweetness and a hint of vanilla, and fall in lovely little pillows that barely stand on their own. It should be just shy of underwhipped—we're not trying to make butter here!

Make this as close as you can to serving, but it can be held in the fridge for two to three hours.

In a stand mixer or working by hand with a whisk, preferably with a chilled bowl, whip the cream with the sugar and vanilla on high speed until soft peaks form.

MAKES 2 CUPS

1 pint heavy cream

2 tablespoons confectioners' sugar

1 teaspoon vanilla extract

### Rhubarb

The thing about rhubarb is that it's always different, depending on the weather, the growing season, and also the variety. Sometimes the rhubarb is a deep ruby color, and other times it's closer to green. You just have to respect it, make good decisions, and work with what you've got. If your base is looking a little green, you can always pink it up with a little beet juice.

**This recipe is like tea and dessert all in one.** As for burning the tops to create that signature caramelized crust, forget those little kitchen torches. I hate them. I went down to Freedom General and bought myself an actual blowtorch. Every girl should have one—that and a power screwdriver.

**SERVES 6**

# Chamomile Crème Brûlée

1 quart heavy cream

1 cup sugar

2 tablespoons honey

¼ cup loose chamomile tea

6 large egg yolks

Bring the cream to a simmer in a medium saucepan over medium heat. Add ½ cup of the sugar, the honey, and tea. Remove from the heat and let the mixture steep for 15 minutes.

Beat the egg yolks in a large bowl.

Strain out the tea, discard, and return the infused cream to the pan. Bring back to a slow boil. Remove from the heat.

Slowly whisk a bit of the cream mixture into the eggs to temper (so the eggs don't scramble when you add the rest of the hot cream mixture). Then slowly whisk in the remaining cream. Pour the hot custard base through a fine-mesh sieve to catch any bits of egg that may have cooked.

Divide the custard among six 6-ounce ramekins or teacups. There will be small bubbles on the surface of each custard after you pour; you can burst these by waving your torch over them to make for a smoother surface. (Or you can leave the bubbles and not worry about them.) Transfer the ramekins to the fridge; I like to let the custard base chill overnight to intensify the flavor. Longer is better, but the world will not end if you let it chill for only 2 hours.

The next day, preheat the oven to 350°F.

Put the ramekins inside a baking dish and pour enough water into the dish to come halfway up the sides of the cups. Cover the dish with foil and carefully transfer it to the oven. Bake until the edges of the custard are set and the center is still a bit jiggly, about 40 minutes. Remove the ramekins from the water bath and let cool completely. Refrigerate until ready to serve.

To serve, sprinkle the remaining ½ cup sugar over the tops of the custards. Shake it around so that it completely and evenly covers the surface; shake off any excess. With a blowtorch on high, hold the flame steady about an inch from the surface of the custard and let the sugar caramelize. Continue until there's a uniform golden crust. Repeat with the rest and serve immediately. Don't worry if it's not perfect—it takes practice!

My Gram wasn't the best cook, but pies were her thing. I can still taste the sugary graham cracker crust she'd press into the tins and then top with creamy vanilla pudding. We'd sell them at the diner, finished off with a mountain of whipped cream and a maraschino cherry. I dress up my version with a spray of Johnny-jump-ups or any other edible flowers I can find.

MAKES 1 (9-INCH) PIE; SERVES 8

# Graham Cracker Pie

MAKE THE CRUST: Preheat the oven to 350°F.

In a food processor, pulse the graham crackers and sugar until well ground. Transfer to a medium bowl and stir in the melted butter until well incorporated. Press the crust mixture into a 9-inch tart pan with a removable bottom. Bake until the crust is set but not yet browned, about 10 minutes, then allow it to cool.

MAKE THE FILLING: Heat the milk, vanilla bean and seeds, sugar, salt, and cornstarch in a medium saucepan over medium heat, whisking constantly until it thickens, 6 to 8 minutes.

In a large bowl, lightly beat the egg yolks. Slowly whisk a bit of the hot milk mixture into the yolks to temper (so the yolks don't scramble when you add the rest of the hot filling). Then slowly whisk in the remaining milk. Return the mixture to the saucepan and whisk constantly over medium heat until it just starts to bubble. Remove from the heat, let cool slightly, and stir in the vanilla.

Pour the filling into the prepared crust and let it set in the refrigerator, at least 4 to 6 hours or overnight. Serve slices topped with whipped cream.

FOR THE CRUST

9 graham crackers
(1 sleeve)

¼ cup sugar

6 tablespoons (¾ stick)
unsalted butter, melted

FOR THE FILLING

3 cups whole milk

1 vanilla bean, split
lengthwise and scraped

⅔ cup sugar

Pinch of salt

¼ cup cornstarch

3 large egg yolks

2 teaspoons vanilla
extract

Perfectly Whipped
Cream (page 62)

These sweets originated in Portland, Maine, and you'd be hard-pressed to find them anywhere else. They're like the Northeastern version of a Mounds bar, with a chocolate shell and a creamy coconut-flavored inside that also features potato, giving it an even denser, richer consistency. My Gram—or Moonie, as everyone else called her—used to send boxes of these to me in college so I'd always have a taste of home. Now I make them substituting parsnips, which have more flavor, for the classic potato.

MAKES ABOUT 65 (1-INCH) BALLS

# Parsnip Needhams

2 medium parsnips, peeled and roughly chopped (about 2 cups)

3 tablespoons unsalted butter, plus more for the pan

1 pound confectioners' sugar

14 ounces unsweetened flaked coconut

2 teaspoons vanilla extract

1 pound bittersweet chocolate

½ cup plus 2 tablespoons coconut oil

Maldon salt

Put the parsnips in a small saucepan with just enough cold water to cover. Bring to a boil, then reduce the heat and simmer until the parsnips are fork-tender, about 10 minutes. Drain, mash until smooth, and set aside to cool. Reserve 1 cup.

Coat one baking sheet with butter and line a second sheet with parchment paper.

In a double boiler or a large heatproof bowl set atop a saucepan of simmering water, combine the 1 cup mashed parsnips, the confectioners' sugar, and butter. Stir constantly until the sugar melts and the mixture is well incorporated. Stir in the flaked coconut and vanilla.

Roll the mixture into 1-inch balls (about a tablespoon each) and arrange on the buttered baking sheet. Refrigerate for about an hour to set.

Melt the chocolate and coconut oil in a double boiler. Whisk until smooth. Remove from the heat.

Dip each ball into the chocolate to coat. Put them on the parchment-lined baking sheet and sprinkle with Maldon salt. Let sit in a cool place until the chocolate sets, 15 to 20 minutes. Store in an airtight container for up to a week.

# Sorbets for All Seasons

**My obsession with sorbets** started when I was hosting the supper club and scraping together to collect dishes and silverware and cooking gear and gadgets and everything else under the sun, even working in a cooking store and handing over every last dime I made for knives and cutting boards and pots and pans. But the one thing that was beyond my reach was an ice cream machine. I daydreamed about all the ways I'd serve sorbet—sweet and savory, herb- and flower-infused, seasonally inspired. Then one day, a friend showed up at my apartment and opened her trunk, revealing the loveliest Italian ice cream maker. She no longer had any need for it and knew that I would give it a good home.

At my dinners, I'd come around with small scoops of savory sorbet on vintage spoons to signal that the four courses were about to start; or I'd use a fresh, herbaceous version as a palate cleanser; or I'd serve sorbet as a dessert in sherbet bowls or egg cups. And now there's not a day at the restaurant that we don't serve sorbet in some way. The best part is that sorbets are incredibly easy to play with once you know how to make a simple syrup.

If you do not own an ice cream machine, you can pour the sorbet mixture into a shallow freezer-safe container and mix it by hand every few hours until frozen and smooth. The results may be a little more granita-like, but they'll still be delicious.

## SPRING

### RHUBARB ELDERFLOWER SORBET

MAKES ABOUT 1 PINT

2 cups chopped rhubarb (about 6 medium stalks), ends trimmed

¼ cup sugar

Grated zest and juice of ½ lemon

1 tablespoon elderflower liqueur (optional)

Simple Syrup (page 73)

Combine the rhubarb, sugar, and lemon zest and juice in a small saucepan and bring to a simmer over medium heat. Cook until tender and soft, about 10 minutes. Remove from the heat and set aside to cool.

Add the liqueur and simple syrup to the rhubarb mixture and stir. Pass the mixture through a fine-mesh sieve and churn in an ice cream maker according to manufacturer's directions.

## SUMMER

### BLUEBERRY–SWEET TEA SORBET

MAKES ABOUT 1 PINT

Double batch of Earl Grey Simple Syrup (page 73)

1 cup blueberries, fresh or frozen

Juice of ½ lemon

Combine all of the ingredients in a blender and blend until smooth. Pass the mixture through a fine-mesh sieve and churn in an ice cream maker according to manufacturer's directions.

## FALL

### APPLE CIDER & ROSEMARY SORBET

**MAKES ABOUT 1 PINT**

Rosemary Simple Syrup (opposite)

2 cups apple cider

Combine the simple syrup and cider, then transfer the mixture to an ice cream maker and churn according to the manufacturer's directions.

## WINTER

### CLEMEN-THYME SORBET

**MAKES ABOUT 1 PINT**

Thyme Simple Syrup (opposite)

2 cups fresh clementine juice

Combine the simple syrup and clementine juice, then transfer the mixture to an ice cream maker and churn according to the manufacturer's directions.

# SIMPLE SYRUP

After bartending for years, I learned how versatile a syrup base can be, whether for making sorbets or cocktails. Just infuse the sugar water with any flavors you can dream up, adjusting the sugar as needed, and store in the fridge for up to a week. If using the syrup for a sorbet, always oversweeten it. It might taste perfect in the pot, but the sweetness tames after it freezes.

**MAKES ¾ CUP**

½ cup sugar

Combine the sugar and ½ cup water in a small saucepan and bring to a boil over medium-high heat. Allow the mixture to boil just long enough for the sugar to dissolve, about 1 minute. Remove the pan from the heat and let cool. Pour into a jar with a lid and refrigerate for up to a week.

### Earl Grey Simple Syrup

Add 2 tablespoons loose Earl Grey tea when you remove the syrup from the heat and let steep for 15 minutes before straining.

### Rosemary Simple Syrup

Add 4 sprigs of fresh rosemary when you remove the syrup from the heat and let steep for 15 minutes before straining.

### Thyme Simple Syrup

Add 6 sprigs of fresh thyme when you remove the syrup from the heat and let steep for 15 minutes before straining.

### Cilantro Simple Syrup

Add ½ cup cilantro leaves and ½ small jalapeño, sliced, when you remove the syrup from the heat and let steep for 15 minutes before straining.

**I worked on this cake for a year.** It actually started as a carrot cake, which people love because it's so comforting and familiar. But I wanted to put a twist on it, make it better. My mind went to spring-dug parsnips, which are the unsung gems of the root vegetable family. Since they're allowed to stay in the ground over the winter, they freeze, which sends their sugar content through the roof. Plus, when I get the call from a farmer that their parsnips are coming up, it means the ground has finally shed its frost and spring is imminent.

Although this combination of flavors might sound unorthodox, people can't get enough of this cake. I get calls to ask whether I'll ship it out of state—it's that good.

**SERVES 8**

# Sweet Parsnip Cake
## WITH HAZELNUTS & MASCARPONE

**MAKE THE CAKE:** Preheat the oven to 375°F. Butter two 10-inch springform pans, line the bottoms with parchment paper, and butter and flour the paper and sides, tapping out excess flour.

Combine the flour, baking powder, baking soda, cinnamon, and salt in a medium bowl.

In a stand mixer fitted with the paddle attachment, combine the vegetable oil, eggs, orange zest and juice, granulated sugar, and brown sugar. Mix on low until smooth. Add the dry ingredients and mix on low speed until just blended, scraping down the sides of the bowl with a spatula as needed. Add the parsnips and hazelnuts and mix until just incorporated.

Divide the batter between the two pans and bake until a cake tester or knife inserted in the center comes out clean, 20 to 25 minutes. Let the cakes cool in the pans on a wire rack.

**FOR THE CAKE**

Unsalted butter, at room temperature, for the pan

2 cups all-purpose flour, plus more for the pan

2 teaspoons baking powder

2 teaspoons baking soda

2 teaspoons ground cinnamon

1 teaspoon salt

¾ cup vegetable oil

4 large eggs

Grated zest and juice of 1 orange

¾ cup granulated sugar

⅔ cup packed light brown sugar

3 cups grated raw parsnips (from 2 to 3 pounds)

1 cup hazelnuts, toasted and roughly chopped

**FOR THE FROSTING**

6 tablespoons (¾ stick) unsalted butter, at room temperature

⅓ cup confectioners' sugar, plus more for dusting

1 (8-ounce) container mascarpone

⅓ cup apricot jam

**MAKE THE FROSTING:** In a stand mixer fitted with the paddle attachment, beat the butter until fluffy and pale, about 1 minute. Add the confectioners' sugar and beat again for another minute. Add the mascarpone and jam and mix until just incorporated.

Remove the sides of the springform pans. Put one of the cakes upside down on a cake stand and remove the parchment paper. Spread the frosting over the cake. Top with the second cake, remove the parchment, and dust with confectioners' sugar. You can refrigerate any leftovers for a day or two, but they won't last that long.

**The only thing that beats an ice cream sundae** is one drizzled with fresh maple syrup—the surest sign that spring is on its way. We're tapping our trees just as the first whispers of warmth creep into winter. Most of it doesn't even make it into a jar; it goes hot from the evaporator to a bowl of ice cream.

SERVES 6

# Maple & Candied Walnut Ice Cream Sundae

2 cups heavy cream

2 cups whole milk

½ cup sugar

1 vanilla bean, split lengthwise and scraped

8 large egg yolks

¾ cup maple syrup, warmed, for serving

1 cup candied walnuts (opposite)

Perfectly Whipped Cream (page 62)

In a medium saucepan over medium heat, combine the cream, milk, sugar, and vanilla bean and seeds. Bring to a slow simmer to allow the sugar to dissolve. Remove the pan from the heat and allow the flavors to infuse for 20 minutes.

Beat the egg yolks in a medium bowl. Slowly pour in the warm cream, whisking constantly. Return the mixture to the saucepan and cook over medium heat, whisking constantly, until the custard has thickened ever so slightly but does not boil, about 4 minutes. Strain the mixture through a fine-mesh sieve and refrigerate until cool, preferably overnight.

Churn the custard in an ice cream maker according to the manufacturer's instructions. Pack the ice cream into freezer-safe containers and freeze until ready to serve.

Serve scoops of ice cream drizzled with warm maple syrup, a sprinkling of candied nuts, and a dollop of whipped cream.

## CANDIED NUTS

These are great on salads, over desserts, and even as a nibble sprinkled with something savory like cayenne, rosemary, or thyme.

Preheat the oven to 375°F. Line a baking sheet with parchment paper.

Combine the sugar with ½ cup water in a small saucepan and bring to a boil. Toss in the nuts, stir to coat, then spread them out on the baking sheet. Bake until toasty, 8 to 10 minutes. Sprinkle with Maldon salt to taste. Set aside to cool.

Store any leftovers in a sealed container in your pantry for up to a month.

MAKES 2 CUPS

½ cup sugar

2 cups nuts, such as walnuts, hazelnuts, pecans, or almonds

Maldon salt

## Maple Trees and Sweet Rewards

In March, when winter softens and spring becomes a glistening notion, the maple trees begin their yearly running of the sap. This clear, slightly sweet, watery liquid may not appear to be anything special, but after a few hours of boiling over a roaring wood fire, the liquid evaporates and leaves behind the caramelized sweet syrup that has become known as the better half of the blueberry pancake. Tapping trees is extremely simple to do, and the satisfaction you get from sopping up the liquid gold that *you* made is edibly priceless. To me, one of the best parts of tapping my own trees is digging out a fire pit in the snow, throwing on a giant pot of non-syrup-bound sap, and boiling some hot dogs.

There are many varieties of maple trees, so you'll want to do a little research to figure out which types thrive in your area. In a pinch, you can use this novice method: while the trees still have their leaves, look for the classic five-lobed maple leaf and mark the tree for later. Here in Maine, sugar maples are the most beloved for collecting sap. They're larger than other maples and therefore have a higher yield. They're also the spookiest-looking trees around with thick, gnarled bases, vertically striped bark, and gangly, twisted branches.

And if you don't live up the road from a sugar shack, like I do, your best bet is to find the spiles and buckets online.

You will need the following tools and items to tap your own maple trees:

- Power screwdriver with a ⅜-inch bit

- Spiles with bucket hooks

- Galvanized sap-collection buckets with covers

- 5-gallon food-grade container (for storage)

Check your sap buckets each day, emptying them into the larger food-grade container as needed. Once you have accumulated about 5 gallons of sap—enough to make roughly 1 pint of syrup—you can begin the boiling process. Ideally this can be done outside over a wood fire, or else you'll end up with really sticky walls.

To make a pint of syrup you will need the following:

- A large stockpot, at least 24-quart

- Fine-mesh sieve

- Cheesecloth

- Instant-read thermometer

- Sterilized glass jar with lid for storing

In the large stockpot over high heat, bring the sap to a boil. Continue boiling until it turns a deep golden brown and reaches a temperature of 219°F, 3 to 4 hours. Line the sieve with cheesecloth, pour the remaining pint of syrup through the sieve into the jar, cover, and refrigerate. The syrup will keep in the fridge for up to 6 months.

# SUMMER

---

SALT, SUN & FIREFLIES

Summer in Maine has its way of bewitching us. The days are longer and the sun is warmer, encouraging us to accomplish as much as we can in this short, sweet season. There is, after all, so much to be done! Gardens to tend, lawns to mow, a bounty from the fields to pickle and preserve. And then, with to-do lists growing, we are inevitably seduced by the pleasures of a Maine summer instead: swimming every day before the waters turn icy and frigid again; harvesting apples, pears, and plums before they fall to the ground and disappear, seemingly within the blink of an eye; dining outside as often as possible to absorb the last precious rays of the warm evening sun and to catch those soft August night breezes that keep the mosquitos away. The crickets chirp louder, the moon rises fuller. These are the days we dream of on cold February nights.

# FIRSTS

Fried Squash Blossoms
Chilled Golden Beet & Buttermilk Soup
Spicy Tomato & Tomatillo Soup
Squid Stuffed with Sausage
Fried Green Tomatoes with Buttermilk & Chives

# MAINS

11-Minute Lobster
Cornflake Fried Chicken with Perfect Potato Salad
Skillet Mussels with Rosemary, Lavender & Lime
Maine Halibut Niçoise
A Classic Clam Boil
Rib Eye Steaks with Herb Butter & Frites
Pork Burgers with Grilled Peaches, Bacon & Blue Cheese
Black Bass with Summer Beans & Bee Balm Bread Salad

# SWEETS

Grilled Stone Fruit, Blue Cheese & Honey
Elderflower Fritters
Summer Berries with Ginger-Cream Shortcakes
Fresh Blueberries with Basil Custard Cream
Peach & Ginger Cobbler
Ripe Cantaloupe & Ruby Port Ice

If you see squash blossoms at the market, buy them without hesitation. They are a fleeting presence, and the perfect delicate vessel for herbed creamy cheeses. I prefer winter squash blossoms because they're heartier and easier to work with, as opposed to more delicate zucchini blossoms.

SERVES 4 TO 8

# Fried Squash Blossoms

Vegetable oil, for frying

1 cup ricotta

⅓ cup grated pecorino

1 tablespoon chopped fresh marjoram

1 tablespoon chopped fresh dill

Grated zest of 1 lemon

Salt

8 squash blossoms, stamens (and any critters) removed

Fresh chives or dill sprigs, for tying

1 cup all-purpose flour

1½ cups sparkling water

Heat oil in a deep fryer to 375°F or, alternatively, heat 2 inches of oil in a heavy-bottomed pan to the same temperature.

In a medium bowl, combine the ricotta, pecorino, marjoram, dill, and lemon zest. Season with salt to taste.

Gently stuff each blossom with enough ricotta mixture to fill it without overstuffing and tearing the delicate leaves. The blossoms range in size, so use your best judgment. Leave enough room at the end of the blossom so you can pull the tips together. Give them a gentle twist to secure and then tie them off with a few long chives. The process takes patience and a bit of grace but is well worth the effort.

In another bowl, make the tempura batter by whisking the flour and sparkling water until smooth.

Working in 2 batches, dip each blossom into the batter. Gently shake off any excess and drop into the hot oil 4 at a time. Do not overcrowd the oil or the temperature will drop and the fritters' coating will get soggy. Fry, turning as needed, until the blossoms are golden brown, 2 to 4 minutes. Remove the fritters with a slotted spoon and transfer to a paper towel to blot any excess grease. Sprinkle with salt. Repeat with the remaining fritters and serve immediately.

**I've always loved playing around** with chilled beet soup, but often my attempts turned out looking like Pepto-Bismol. But then I tried it with a bag of golden beets from a local farm, added buttermilk, and got the most beautiful sunshine yellow color—like marigolds in a bowl. This soup is tangy, cool, and refreshing.

SERVES 6

# Chilled Golden Beet & Buttermilk Soup

I like to boil beets over medium heat in well-salted water as opposed to roasting them—it keeps them juicy and flavorful. Put the beets in a large pot, add just enough cold water to cover, season well with salt, and bring to a boil. Cook until tender, 25 to 40 minutes, depending on their size. Remove the beets, allow them to cool to room temperature, then peel off the skins with your hands.

Cut 1 beet into small dice about the size of your pinky nail. In a small bowl, toss the beet with the macerated shallot vinaigrette and set aside. Cut the rest of the beets into large chunks.

Puree the chopped beets, buttermilk, and lemon juice in a blender until smooth. Season with salt and pepper to taste. Refrigerate for at least 1 hour or until completely cooled.

Ladle the soup into bowls and drizzle with olive oil. Put the dill fronds and basil leaves in a small ramekin and the sour cream in a second ramekin. Serve along with the marinated beets so people can garnish their soups as desired.

2½ pounds golden beets (about 8 medium)

Salt and pepper

1 tablespoon Macerated Shallot Vinaigrette (page 30)

2 cups buttermilk

Juice of ½ lemon

Olive oil, for drizzling

3 tablespoons snipped dill fronds

3 tablespoons small basil leaves

¼ cup sour cream

This soup is inspired by my friend Victoria, whose gardens reflect her personality. Coming to Maine by way of California—where she learned to love all things spicy—she grows all manner of peppers, plus cilantro, tomatoes, and tomatillos, which you rarely see this far north. She's also a vegetarian, so I wanted to come up with something that would use the produce she grows. This soup is simple and raw—everything goes into the blender with a little olive oil, rice wine vinegar, and salt, and there you have it. For Victoria, with love.

SERVES 6

# Spicy Tomato & Tomatillo Soup

In a blender, puree the tomatoes, tomatillos, garlic, cilantro, jalapeño, olive oil, and vinegar until smooth. Season to taste with salt and pepper. Strain through a fine-mesh sieve. Chill for at least 1 hour.

2 pounds tomatoes, the freshest, most beautiful ones you can find, quartered

1 pound tomatillos, husks removed

2 garlic cloves

4 sprigs of fresh cilantro

1 jalapeño

¼ cup olive oil

2 tablespoons rice wine vinegar

Salt and pepper

**Stuffing squid is a no-brainer.** Their bodies even look like sausage casings. You just put in your stuffing, brown the squid in a cast-iron skillet, and finish them off in the oven—or do them on the grill. I serve them with spicy mustard greens and Chinese mustard for a kick.

For the sausage, buy fresh, homemade sausage from your butcher or at your farmer's market. Go with a flavor that you love.

**SERVES 6 TO 8**

# Squid Stuffed with Sausage

Preheat the oven to 425°F.

Make the vinaigrette by whisking together 3 tablespoons of the olive oil, the vinegar, mustard, and shallot. Season to taste with salt and pepper and set aside.

Gently stuff each squid body with about a tablespoon of sausage.

Heat the remaining tablespoon olive oil in a large ovenproof skillet, preferably cast iron, over medium-high heat. When the oil starts to smoke, add the squid bodies and cook, turning once, until just golden brown, about 2 minutes per side.

Add the tentacles to the skillet along with the butter. Transfer the pan to the oven and roast until the sausage is cooked through, 6 to 8 minutes.

Toss the greens with the vinaigrette and serve with the hot squid, along with mustard for dipping.

¼ cup olive oil

1 tablespoon seasoned rice wine vinegar

1 teaspoon Dijon mustard

1 tablespoon finely chopped shallot

Salt and pepper

1 pound cleaned fresh squid (about a dozen bodies and tentacles), rinsed under cold water

1 pound fresh sausage, removed from casing if not loose

3 tablespoons unsalted butter

½ pound young mustard greens

Prepared mustard, preferably Chinese spicy

**Buying Squid**

Always buy fresh squid. If you can't find them fresh, don't use them (seriously, don't!). Ideally have your fishmonger clean them because that job is a pain in the butt.

**This recipe is made for when** the tomatoes aren't quite ripe but you just can't wait any longer.

SERVES 6

# Fried Green Tomatoes
## WITH BUTTERMILK & CHIVES

Heat oil in a deep fryer to 375°F or, alternatively, heat 2 inches of oil in a heavy-bottomed pan to the same temperature.

In a small bowl, make the buttermilk dressing by whisking together the mayo, sour cream, 2 tablespoons of the buttermilk, and 1 tablespoon of the dill. Season (liberally) with salt and pepper to taste.

Slice the tomatoes into ¼-inch-thick rounds. Put them in a medium bowl with the remaining 2 cups buttermilk and a pinch each of salt and pepper.

In a separate bowl, stir together the flour and semolina.

Dredge the tomato rounds in the flour mixture to thoroughly coat. Drop them into the oil 4 to 6 at a time. Do not overcrowd the oil or the temperature will drop and the coating will get soggy. Fry, turning as needed, until the tomatoes are golden brown, 3 to 4 minutes. Remove the tomatoes with a slotted spoon and transfer to paper towels to blot any excess grease. Sprinkle with the remaining chopped dill and drizzle with the buttermilk dressing. Garnish with edible flowers, if desired.

Vegetable oil, for frying

¼ cup mayonnaise, homemade (page 37) or store-bought

¼ cup sour cream

2 cups plus 2 tablespoons buttermilk

3 tablespoons chopped fresh dill

Salt and pepper

4 green tomatoes

1 cup all-purpose flour

1 cup semolina flour

Gem marigolds, for garnish (optional)

## Roadside Rummaging

Living in Maine has made me frugal. I pay close attention to nature, the seasons, and the free wild goods that are all around me. I hunt, fish, forage, pickle, and preserve my way through summer. I have no shame when it comes to pulling over on any given roadside, jumping through wet ditches, and pushing my way through puckerbrush to get some juniper to throw into a skillet of steaming mussels, elderflowers to steep into a cordial, or nutty wild sunchokes for a silky soup. (Thanks, Mom, for making me keep a good pair of boots, pruning shears, and a basket in the back of my car—because you never know what you may find along your travels!)

These are some of my favorite items to forage. Come late spring and early summer, they're fresh, free, and completely unfussy.

- **Milkweed shoots:** Enjoy them when they're only 3 to 4 inches tall, before they've really sprouted their leaves. Roast like asparagus.

- **Queen Anne's lace:** The original carrot. The roots can be shaved and tossed into salads or cooked into jam. Sprinkle the blossoms anywhere you would edible flowers, or use in floral arrangements.

- **Spruce tips:** Little green shoots that emerge right at the beginning of the season and have an earthy but sweet, piney flavor. Throw them into Skillet Mussels with Rosemary, Lavender & Lime (page 107), make a simple syrup with them for cocktails or sorbets, or use for a custard or ice cream.

- **Fiddleheads:** Sauté (see Ramp & Fiddlehead Fried Rice, page 40), pickle, or batter and fry.

- **Ramps:** Same as above, plus you can fold them into butter and slather on steak, grill them whole, or pickle and toss into a Gibson.

- **Purslane:** This weed growing through the garden path is more succulent than a delicate green and has a tart, almost lemon-like taste. Throw into salads or give a quick char on the grill.

- **Sunchokes:** Wake up early to collect these tubers, so the neighbor's dogs aren't awake yet. Use the roots to make creamy soups, hash, or potato salad, and use the flowers—which taste just like the roots—to top salads or to make a pretty floral arrangement.

- **Dandelion greens:** A delicious bitter green that's in just about everyone's yard. Sauté with garlic and lemon.

- **Sea rose:** Out en masse along the water in August, these blossoms have a beautiful beachy, floral scent. Use them to make a quintessentially summer gin and tonic (see page 145) or cook into jams, jellies, syrups, sorbet, or ice cream.

- **Day lilies:** Sauté the pods with olive oil, butter, salt, and pepper; use the petals in salads or spring rolls; or include the roots anywhere you would jicama or radishes.

- **Elderflowers:** Great for cordials and fritters (see pages 130 and 131). Don't eat them raw.

- **Juniper berries:** Juniper is really nice for steaming in pots of mussels and infusing into a brine. It also makes a beautiful garnish, especially for poultry. I describe its aroma and flavor as "hippy peppercorn."

## A Foraging Caveat

In the summer of 2013 I took to the roads of Maine in a vintage Airstream, turning out pop-up suppers in fields, barns, and greenhouses. I was lucky enough to land a weekend gig at Four Season Farm, home of Eliot Coleman. If going back to the land could be considered fashionable, Eliot Coleman would be the Anna Wintour of farming. He is primarily known for his organic, year-round gardening in the harsh Maine climate, and his homestead sits on sixty acres of beautiful farmland in the sweet peninsula town of Harborside.

In a borrowed Ford truck, Airstream in tow, my ten-year-old son Jaim and I made our way over pine-studded roads, passing fields of swaying goldenrod, rounding rocky coves, and rolling through blueberry barrens before coming to the little dirt drive leading us to the famous farm. I parked my rig beside a sprawling field of Tuscan kale and fell asleep as lists for tomorrow's dinner reeled through my mind.

I awoke early the next morning to prepare. I would take in the land, forage and scavenge, and then create with my findings. I walked barefoot along the beach—the coastal Maine perfection that "Wish You Were Here" postcards and children's storybooks are made of (seriously, it's what inspired all the Robert McCloskey books)—filling my basket with wild mustard beans for salad, sea heather for cocktails, and rose hips for jam. Jaim and I dug for clams and skipped flat rocks along the calm August waves. I pulled wild purple thistle and bright pink sea roses from the roadside to fill giant vases. Then, out of the corner of my eye, I spotted these amazing tall twigs with lime green

baubles . . . the perfect complement to my arrangement. Still barefoot, I parted the hedge of roadside weeds, pushed through the bramble, and with the pruning shears in my back pocket, harvested half a dozen stalks of this foraged gold.

Back at the farm, before I set forth playing with my newfound goods, I stuffed a giant clear vase with the stalks I'd collected, lovingly pruning the shiny leaves around the green berry-like clusters.

My kitchen help for the evening began to arrive and jumped into last-minute prep work—arranging cheese platters for cocktail hour and filling little brown bags with gingersnap cookies that our guests would later take home.

"That's quite an arrangement!" exclaimed my friend Anne. "Is it a joke?"

"Thanks!" I replied. "Wait, what do you mean?"

"Erin, it's poison ivy!"

Having spent my formative years rustling through all manner of foliage—and having to deal with the bubbling red rash that results from unsure footing—I knew what poison ivy looked like. But, as Anne assured me, this was how it looked up in these parts.

My face burned, though more from the embarrassment that yes, I had indeed harvested gigantic stalks of poison ivy for my dinner guests—Eliot Coleman and his expert gardener wife, Barbara Damrosch—to enjoy. Needless to say, though, my skin was more in need of balm than my pride.

Unfortunately, you can't just wash away the toxic oils from a poison ivy plant. The resulting skin blisters simply have to pass. It takes time to get over, but eventually the scars heal and the pain is but a distant memory. Kind of like a bad relationship.

### Learn to identify poison ivy:
The basic rule of thumb is: "Leaves of three, let it be." However, it's not ironclad. Before foraging, make sure you acquaint yourself with the shape it takes in your area.

### To help soothe a poison ivy rash:
This magic elixir is what my grandmother doused me with after I had gotten into a patch of PI. There was always a jar on hand under her kitchen sink.

YOU WILL NEED:

Orange jewelweed (that invasive weed that grows in your flower beds and along the roadsides)

Witch hazel

Roughly chop the jewelweed (stalk, leaves, and all) and fill a 1-pint wide-mouth Mason jar. Cover with witch hazel and secure the lid. Store in a cool, dark place for about a week. Strain the jewelweed from the witch hazel and discard, saving the liquid. Dab on poison ivy with a clean cotton ball for relief. It will both tame the itch and dry out the rash.

**I rarely serve lobster** in the restaurant because I don't see the point of eating it any other way than steamed and dipped in butter. Why step on the feet of perfection? All you need is a big pot, salted water, and eleven minutes.

This method is suited for a 1¼- to 1½-pound lobster (not the 2- or 3-pounders, which you don't want anyway because they're tougher and more rubbery). Buy the freshest lobsters you can find; they should be lively, not droopy. When you hold them upside down, their claws should move and the tail should flap. They can live for a couple days in the fridge. Most places will give you the choice of hard- or soft-shell lobster. Hard-shell lobsters have more meat than the lesser-known soft-shell ones, but the soft-shells have sweeter meat. I'd rather have to order two and have the sweeter meat!

SERVES 4

½ cup salt

4 lobsters (1¼ to 1½ pounds each)

Lemon wedges

Melted butter

Apple cider vinegar

# 11-Minute Lobster

Fill a lobster pot (or a stockpot big enough to hold 4 lobsters) about three-quarters full with water, add the salt, and bring to a boil. Add the lobsters to the pot—remember to remove the big rubber bands from the claws, because who wants to eat boiled rubber?—and cover. Cook for 11 minutes over high heat.

Remove the lobsters with tongs and lay them on a platter. Serve with cracking utensils, lemon wedges, and little bowls of melted butter and apple cider vinegar.

**Lobster Finished on the Grill**

If you find yourself with a roaring fire on the beach—or with a nice, hot grill—you can give the lobsters a smoky finish. I particularly like doing this because the fire helps melt off any tomalley. Just take the lobsters out of the boiling water at the 8-minute mark, halve them lengthwise, brush the flesh with melted butter, and put them flesh-side down on the grate. Cook for 3 minutes and serve.

## Lobster Without Intimidation

Tucking into a hard-shell lobster can be tricky, and the only way to get good at it is to do it often. Bottom line: people need to eat more lobster.

- First, eating lobster is not a dainty effort, so don't worry about getting dirty, and have plenty of cloths at the table along with a big platter for shells. And don't take a phone call—you leave a claw on your plate and walk away, it won't be there when you come back.

- Look for the big joints on the lobster and, with one end in each hand, bend or twist them in opposite directions so they meet resistance.

- Start with the claws by separating them from where they meet the body. Carefully bend back the small loose part of the claw to remove it (the thumb, if you will), then use a lobster cracker or hammer to crack the large section of claw. Pry the two sides apart and remove the meat. Continue cracking the joints for the arm and removing the meat with either your fingers or a small "picker."

- Gently twist the body and tail to disconnect them. Then put both your hands on the tail and squeeze so the shell cracks and you can pry it open to pull out the meat.

- You may come across some green goop or "tomalley," which is a lobster's digestive system. It's edible, but it's also where any pollution a lobster takes in through its diet is concentrated. There also could be some bright-red stuff, which is roe, or unfertilized eggs, in a female lobster. This is also edible.

- Remove all the smaller legs from the body and suck out the meat.

- Pry the top shell off the body like you would the hood of a car. You can save the shell for stock or discard. Remove the fuzzy-looking middle section (the gills or circulation system). Herein lies the "secret meat." Just dig your fingers through the cartilage and pick out the shards of meat. It's more like crab-picking, but there's no sense in wasting it.

- Finally, if you're having a lobster feed, you're bound to have leftovers. Save them to fold into scrambled eggs for lobster omelets; drizzle with warmed butter or toss with mayonnaise and stuff into a buttered, grilled hot dog bun for lobster rolls; or toss into pastas, salads, or soups.

**Sometimes it's best not to mess with a classic**—though I do love adding an unconventional sweet-and-sour dipping sauce. Eat this chicken hot out of the fryer or pack it up for a picnic and have it cold.

I never buy cheap ingredients, but trust me, the key to this recipe is the cheap-o cornflakes. Save the fancy organic ones for eating at breakfast with a drizzle of honey and raw milk. Do not use them here.

**SERVES 4**

# Cornflake Fried Chicken
## WITH PERFECT POTATO SALAD

1 chicken (3 to 4 pounds) cut into 10 parts (see page 232)

Basic Brine (page 170)

4 cups all-purpose flour

4 cups cornflakes

Vegetable oil, for frying

2 cups buttermilk

Salt

Blueberry Sweet & Sour Sauce (page 106)

Perfect Potato Salad (page 106)

Combine the chicken and cooled brine in a large pot and refrigerate overnight.

Bring the chicken in the brine to a simmer over medium heat and cook until the chicken is just cooked through, about 20 minutes. Remove the chicken from the brine and allow to cool. Discard the brine.

Make the batter by combining 2 cups of the flour and the cereal in a gallon-sized plastic bag. Seal the bag and use your hands to crush the flakes and mix them with the flour.

Heat oil in a deep fryer to 375°F or, alternatively, heat 2 inches of oil in a heavy-bottomed pan to the same temperature.

Put the remaining 2 cups flour in a shallow baking dish. Pour the buttermilk into a second shallow baking dish. Pour the cornflake mixture into a third baking dish. Dredge each piece of chicken in the flour, then the buttermilk, and finally the cornflake mixture to coat well. Working in batches, drop into the oil and fry until golden brown, turning as needed, 5 to 6 minutes. Take care not to overcrowd the pan or fryer; cook only 3 or 4 pieces at a time.

Remove the chicken from the oil, blot on paper towels, and sprinkle with salt. Serve with the blueberry sauce and potato salad.

## BLUEBERRY SWEET & SOUR SAUCE

Combine the sugar, vinegar, ketchup, and cornstarch in a small saucepan with 1⅓ cups water and bring to a boil over medium heat. Cook, stirring constantly, until bubbly and thick, about 5 minutes. Stir in the fruit and set aside to cool. Cover and refrigerate for up to 1 week.

MAKES 1½ PINTS

1½ cups sugar

⅔ cup seasoned rice wine vinegar

2 tablespoons ketchup

¼ cup cornstarch

1 cup blueberries or other fruit such as blackberries or chopped peaches

## PERFECT POTATO SALAD

The key to a perfect potato salad—as with all cooking—is having the best ingredients. When you stumble upon the most precious baby potatoes, especially like the ones my dear Victoria grows for me, it's time to make potato salad.

Then, instead of making a heavy, mayonnaise-y salad, toss just-tender potatoes with olive oil, macerated shallot vinaigrette, and whatever green herbs you can get your hands on. I call for dill here, but feel free to substitute anything else light and fresh, such as chives, thyme, or marjoram.

SERVES 8

3 pounds baby potatoes

Salt and pepper

¼ cup Macerated Shallot Vinaigrette (page 30)

1 bunch of fresh dill, chopped

¼ cup olive oil, or more to taste

Put the potatoes in a large pot, add just enough cold water to cover, season well with salt, and bring to a boil. Reduce the heat and simmer until the potatoes are just tender when pierced with a knife. Cooking time will depend on the size of the potatoes, so don't go too far from the stove, and check them frequently. Drain the potatoes and let them cool to room temperature.

Halve or quarter the potatoes into bite-sized pieces. If you're really lucky, you'll find potatoes so small they don't need to be cut up.

Toss the potatoes with the shallots, dill, and olive oil, adding more oil if needed—you want a nice, moist salad. Season with salt and pepper to taste.

**This dish is about to become** an all-time favorite entertaining staple of yours. It's got just five ingredients and one pan, and yet it's pure flavor—not to mention a very sexy plate of food (and how I wooed my boyfriend!). You're eating out of the skillet, picking out the mussels, slathering them with sauce, sopping up the whole mess with good bread (a must), juices running down your face. It's a dish made for conversation. If you can swing it, cook it over a wood fire—it will add a whole other layer of flavor.

SERVES 2

# Skillet Mussels
## WITH ROSEMARY, LAVENDER & LIME

2 pounds mussels, cleaned (see page 108)

4 sprigs of fresh rosemary

1 small handful of fresh lavender

8 tablespoons (1 stick) unsalted butter

2 limes, halved

Over a hot fire, or high heat on your stove, heat a large dry skillet, preferably cast iron. Dump in the mussels in a single layer and top with the rosemary and lavender. Let the pan sit undisturbed, uncovered, until the mussels begin to open their shells, 1½ to 2 minutes.

Dot the butter around the skillet and begin to shake it back and forth over the heat. It will sizzle and smoke as the butter melts. Continue to shake the skillet until the mussels are fully open, 1 to 2 minutes.

Remove the pan from the heat, squeeze the lime halves over the mussels, and serve immediately, in the skillet, with a serving spoon.

## Buying and Caring for Mussels

Look for mussels that are small, black, and glistening; they shouldn't be sitting all dried out in a case. Shells with gray, silver, and blue running through them are old boys that we call "silver backs." They're not going to be as sweet, tender, or briny as younger mussels.

When you get home, the first thing you want to do is rinse them in very cold water or immerse them in a bowl of ice water. Then go through them one by one. The cold water should make their shells shut tightly. If you find any that aren't shut—or that are broken or cracked—discard them. They may open back up when air hits them, and that's fine; that's what they do. At the restaurant we have a rule: when in doubt, throw it out. As you're checking the mussels, remove their beards. Find any small hairy-looking piece sticking from the joint of the shell, then pull and twist at the same time. It should come off fairly easily. Put the prepped mussels in a dry bowl, cover it with a damp towel, and refrigerate. You want them to stay alive until it's time to cook. Never cover live shellfish tightly—they're alive; they need to breathe.

**This version of a classic southern French dish** takes on the flavor of Maine at the height of summer. Tomato season is in full swing, green beans are bountiful, lettuce is everywhere, and the tender new potatoes are just starting to come in.

This dish also showcases my favorite—and foolproof—method for cooking fish. It really started as a necessity, since my little apartment kitchen didn't have any ventilation and the oven was the best place to contain a smoking skillet. But it's become a way to make perfect flaky, moist fish every time. I start by searing it in a pan, then transfer it to the oven. The high heat gives it a nice, crispy crust; then the more even heat of the oven gently finishes the job. And, of course, basting with butter as it cooks doesn't hurt!

SERVES 4

# Maine Halibut Niçoise

Preheat the oven to 425°F.

Put the potatoes in a large pot and cover with water. Season generously with salt and bring to a boil. Reduce the heat so that the water simmers and cook the potatoes until fork-tender, 20 to 25 minutes. Drain and let cool to room temperature. Cut into quarters.

In a small bowl, toss the potatoes, green beans, and tomato with enough of the macerated shallot vinaigrette to coat the vegetables. Season with salt and pepper to taste.

Heat a large ovenproof skillet, preferably cast iron, over high heat, pour in the olive oil, and swirl to coat the bottom of the pan. Season the halibut on both sides with salt and pepper and add it to the hot skillet, skin-side down. You'll know the pan is hot enough when you can hold your hand about 6 inches above it for only 3 seconds. Or the oil will begin to smoke. Be sure there's at least a couple inches of space between the fillets or the fish will steam. Cook in 2 separate pans or in 2 batches, if necessary.

1 pound baby or new potatoes

Salt and pepper

½ pound green beans, blanched (see page 31)

1 large heirloom tomato, sliced into 8 wedges

Macerated Shallot Vinaigrette (page 30)

2 tablespoons olive oil

4 halibut fillets (about ½ pound each)

2 tablespoons unsalted butter

1 head Bibb lettuce, leaves separated

4 large eggs, poached (see page 38)

¼ cup Tapenade (page 112)

1 lemon, quartered

Edible flowers, for garnish (optional)

*(recipe continues)*

Let the fish cook undisturbed until it releases easily from the pan, 2 to 3 minutes. Flip the fish over, add the butter to the pan, and put the pan in the oven. Roast until the fish is just cooked through and golden brown, 4 to 5 minutes, depending on the fillets' thickness. About halfway through the cooking, pull out the pan to baste the fish with the butter and check for doneness. When cooked, the flesh will feel slightly firm and will begin to flake and separate a bit.

Transfer the fish to a plate and allow it to rest for a few moments. Be sure to reserve any pan juices.

Divide the lettuce among 4 plates, arranging it in a small circle. Top each with a small mound of potatoes, green beans, and tomatoes. Give each person a halibut steak and drizzle it with any remaining pan juice. Top each halibut with a poached egg, followed by a spoonful of tapenade. Squeeze a lemon wedge over each plate and garnish with edible flowers, if desired. Tuck in immediately.

## TAPENADE

Combine the olives, anchovy, garlic, and parsley leaves in a food processor. Pulse until the mixture is coarsely chopped. Add the olive oil and lemon juice and pulse again until just combined.

MAKES ABOUT 1 CUP

1 cup pitted Greek olives (I like a mix of kalamata and green olives)

1 anchovy fillet, in oil

1 garlic clove

2 sprigs of flat-leaf parsley, leaves picked

2 tablespoons olive oil

1 teaspoon fresh lemon juice

## Nasturtiums & Other Edible Flowers

One of my earliest memories dates back to when I was four years old and at my grandparents' house. Their driveway was lined with whiskey barrels filled with red and orange nasturtiums, and while I don't know what it was about them that beckoned "eat me," I recall stuffing handfuls of these bright blossoms into my mouth after my grandmother had gone into the house. When she came back out to the yard, though, I immediately dropped the flowers behind my back, confident I was in trouble. She only laughed and assured me that eating these delicate but spicy blooms was not just okay, but encouraged. Then she grabbed a handful for herself, and we happily munched.

I love using edible blooms such as nasturtiums or calendula as a garnish or tossing them into salads. They're as delicious as they are beautiful.

Summer is meant for lazy days, not sweating over hosting a party for friends and family. My friends and I are all about celebrating whatever happens to be in season, showing up at each other's gatherings with eggplants or tomatoes or other gems from our gardens, a bottle of sparkling rosé under an arm. We also love acting like tourists every now and then and throwing a clam boil. We can't help craving some clams, corn with butter, and of course, blueberries for dessert!

Clam boils—or tossing potatoes, onions, hot dogs, sausage, corn, and clams into one big pot and letting them cook together—are perfect for a crowd. Just set out the pot, a giant ladle, a stack of bowls, and let people go for it.

**SERVES 10**

# A Classic Clam Boil

Salt

5 pounds baby red potatoes

2 pounds small shallots

1 bunch of fresh thyme

4 bay leaves

10 hot dogs

10 breakfast sausages

10 pounds clams

10 ears of corn

1 pound butter, melted, for dipping

Fill a GIANT lobster pot (seriously, the biggest one you can find) half full with water and ¼ cup salt (or do what I do and just use seawater). Bring to a boil, then reduce the heat so that the water simmers. Add the potatoes, shallots, thyme, and bay leaves. Cover and cook for 5 minutes.

Remove the lid and layer in the ingredients as follows: hot dogs, sausages, clams, corn. Cover and cook until the clams begin to open, 10 to 15 minutes.

Turn off the heat and serve immediately. Allow guests to serve themselves with a ladle and spoon. Serve with ramekins of melted butter so everyone can have her own.

**Sometimes a girl needs a steak.** And when she does, I recommend slathering a big, juicy, wood-kissed rib eye with herb-infused butter and serving it up with lavender fries.

SERVES 2

# Rib Eye Steaks
## WITH HERB BUTTER & FRITES

Remove the steaks from the fridge and allow them to come to room temperature, about 30 minutes.

Meanwhile, make the herb butter. In a stand mixer with the paddle attachment or a large bowl with a wooden spoon, whip the butter until pale and light. Add ½ teaspoon salt, the marjoram, dill, thyme, and lemon zest. Transfer the butter to a small sheet of parchment paper and use the paper to roll the butter into a small log. Refrigerate until firm.

Prepare the grill (see page 51) or heat a large cast-iron pan or grill pan over medium-high heat on the stove.

Brush the steaks with just enough olive oil to coat and sprinkle generously with salt and pepper. Put the steaks on the grill or in the pan. Turn the steaks every 2 minutes or so until they are nicely browned and cooked to your liking, about 8 minutes total for medium-rare, 130°F to 135°F. Allow the steaks to rest on a platter for a few minutes before serving.

Remove the herb butter from the fridge, slice off a few rounds, and dot them on the resting steaks. Platter up with a good handful of frites and enjoy.

2 (14-ounce) rib eye steaks

8 tablespoons (1 stick) unsalted butter, at room temperature

Salt and pepper

1 teaspoon chopped fresh marjoram

1 teaspoon chopped fresh dill

½ teaspoon chopped fresh thyme

1 teaspoon grated lemon zest

Olive oil

Lavender Frites (page 120)

## LAVENDER FRITES

Adding edible lavender to French fries makes a more interesting frite. Serve these with steaks, burgers, or fried chicken. (Why not? You already have the fryer going …)

Heat vegetable oil in a deep fryer to 325°F or, alternatively, heat 2 inches of oil in a heavy-bottomed pan to the same temperature.

Combine the garlic and olive oil in a small bowl. Set aside.

Fill a large bowl with cold water. Using a mandoline with a large-tooth blade—or a very sharp knife—slice the potatoes into fry-sized logs and put them in the water. Precise measurements aren't as important as uniformity. Let them sit in the water for 20 minutes.

Drain the potatoes and, working in 3 or 4 batches, fry them in the oil until just cooked through but not brown (this will keep them nice and soft on the inside and crispy on the outside), 4 or 5 minutes. Take care not to overcrowd the oil or the fries will steam and get soggy.

Transfer the fries to paper towels and raise the oil temperature to 375°F. (You can test if the oil is ready by dropping a piece of potato into it; the potato should bubble and then brown within 30 to 40 seconds.)

Again in batches, refry the potatoes until golden brown, about 2 minutes. Transfer them to clean paper towels to drain and then to a large bowl. Toss the frites with the reserved garlic and oil, lavender, thyme, and herbes de Provence. Season with a good amount of salt.

SERVES 4 (OR 1)

Vegetable oil, for frying

1 large or 2 small garlic cloves, crushed

1 teaspoon olive oil

1½ pounds mixed Yukon Gold and red potatoes

2 teaspoons fresh lavender flowers

1 teaspoon fresh thyme leaves

2 tablespoons dried herbes de Provence

Salt

**I grew up flipping burgers.** At fourteen years old I was standing in front of a giant flattop covered in patties—including the 1-pound Super Burgers that all the farmhands would order—and learning how to cook them perfectly medium-rare, using only my hands to gauge their temperature.

This one is all about summer. I just love the combo of juicy sweet peaches with smoky bacon and savory blue cheese. And while the homemade poppy seed buns are not a must, I recommend trying them at least once.

**MAKES 6 BURGERS**

# Pork Burgers
## WITH GRILLED PEACHES, BACON & BLUE CHEESE

2½ pounds ground pork

Salt and pepper

2 ripe but firm peaches, halved and cut into thick slices

Olive oil

6 poppy seed buns, homemade (opposite) or store-bought

1 cup mayonnaise, homemade (page 37) or store-bought

6 slices of bacon, cooked

½ pound good blue cheese, cut into chunks

½ pound arugula

Prepare the grill (see page 51).

Portion the pork into 6 patties roughly 1½ inches thick and season generously with salt and pepper. Cook the burgers on the cooler side of the grill for 6 minutes on the first side, 5 minutes on the other (for medium, which I like for pork). Remove the burgers from the grill and let rest for about 5 minutes.

Meanwhile, brush the peach slices with olive oil and grill, turning once, until you get nice grill marks, 3 to 4 minutes total.

Split the buns and grill to toast them, then slather with mayonnaise and stuff each with a patty, a couple of peach slices, bacon, cheese, and arugula.

# POPPY SEED BUNS

Because I love burgers (and who doesn't, really?), I wanted to make a bun that would do them justice. These perfectly doughy, slightly sweet buns are just that. This recipe makes a dozen buns, but you can freeze any leftovers. Butter and grill them or toast them for egg sandwiches in the morning. I love having some of these in the freezer in a pinch.

Gently warm the milk and cream in a small saucepan over low heat. You want the mixture to be just warm, not hot. If it's too hot, it will kill the yeast.

Meanwhile, stir together the warm water, 2 tablespoons of the sugar, and the yeast in a stand mixer fitted with the dough hook or in a large bowl and let sit until foamy, about 5 minutes. (If the mixture doesn't foam, start over with new yeast.)

Add the warm milk mixture, remaining 2 tablespoons sugar, flour, and salt to the yeast mixture and mix on low speed or by hand with a wooden spoon until the flour is incorporated. Increase the speed to medium and beat for 5 minutes or knead by hand on a lightly floured surface. The dough should be slightly sticky but smooth and form a ball; add a bit more flour if the mixture is too wet.

Lightly grease a large bowl with olive oil and turn the dough in the bowl to coat with oil. Cover the bowl with a kitchen towel and let it rise until doubled in size, about 1 hour.

Punch down the dough—seriously, give it a good whack—then roll it out on a floured surface to 1½ inches thick. Cut out 12 buns with a 2-inch round biscuit cutter. Arrange the buns 2 inches apart on a baking sheet lined with parchment paper or a Silpat. Set them aside to rise until doubled in size, at least an hour.

Preheat the oven to 375°F.

Brush the buns with beaten egg and sprinkle with poppy seeds. Bake until the tops are golden and undersides are golden brown, 20 to 25 minutes. Let cool on the pan.

MAKES 1 DOZEN BUNS

1¼ cups whole milk

1 cup heavy cream

¼ cup warm water (105°F to 115°F)

¼ cup sugar

2¼ teaspoons yeast

5 cups all-purpose flour, plus more as needed

2 teaspoons salt

Olive oil

1 large egg, lightly beaten

2 tablespoons poppy seeds

**If it's hot, I'm hankering for this dish.** It's light, fresh, and a welcome departure from giant pieces of meat. Everything gets served at room temperature, and there's no slaving away over a hot stove for hours—just long enough to sear the fish. Then there's the toasted bread to sop up an oily, vinegary dressing until it's barely submitted to softness by the honeysuckle sweetness of bee balm. You're obviously not going to find bee balm in the store—it'll be in your garden or your friends' gardens, but you can use other edible flowers in their place (which you can now find at some stores).

SERVES 4

# Black Bass
## WITH SUMMER BEANS & BEE BALM BREAD SALAD

6 tablespoons olive oil

2 cups cubed good bread

½ pound thin green beans or haricots verts, blanched (see page 31)

2 tablespoons Macerated Shallot Vinaigrette (page 30)

4 sprigs of fresh dill, roughly chopped

Grated zest of ½ lemon

Salt and pepper

4 bee balm blossoms or other edible blossoms (optional)

4 black sea bass fillets (6 to 8 ounces each)

4 tablespoons (½ stick) unsalted butter

Lemon wedges

Preheat the oven to 425°F.

Start by making the bread salad. Heat 1 tablespoon of the olive oil in a large skillet, preferably cast iron, over medium heat. Toss in the bread cubes and toast, continually shaking the pan, until the bread is golden on all sides, about 4 minutes. Stir in the beans, macerated shallot vinaigrette, 3 more tablespoons of the olive oil, the dill, and lemon zest. Season with salt and pepper. Transfer the mixture to a platter and garnish with the bee balm petals, if desired.

Next, cook the fish. Wipe out the skillet and heat the remaining 2 tablespoons olive oil over high heat. Season the fish with salt and pepper. When the oil begins to smoke, gently lay the fish in the skillet, skin-side down. Cook for 1 minute, flip the fish, and add the butter. Transfer the pan to the oven and cook until the fish is firm and just cooked through, 3 to 4 minutes. Baste the fish with the melted butter from the pan.

Serve the fish fillets over the salad with a squeeze of lemon.

**When you can't decide** between a dessert and a cheese course, make this dish. It's a little savory, a little sweet, and perfectly balanced—and just the thing when the grill's been fired up all day but you're not quite ready to let those nice, hot coals go. If blue cheese is not your flavor, fresh ricotta would be equally lovely here.

**SERVES 4**

# Grilled Stone Fruit, Blue Cheese & Honey

4 stone fruits such as apricots, peaches, or plums, halved and pitted

Olive oil

1 teaspoon Maldon salt

1 small wedge (about ¼ pound) best-quality blue cheese

¼ cup best-quality honey

Small basil leaves

Prepare the grill (see page 51) if it isn't already fired up for the main course.

Brush the fruit halves with olive oil and sprinkle with salt. Put them flesh-side down on a hot grill and cook just until you get some good grill marks on the fruit, about 4 minutes. Turn the fruit and grill for another 2 minutes.

Transfer the fruit to a platter, garnish with a bit of blue cheese, a drizzle of honey, and a sprinkling of basil and serve.

**In Freedom, elderflowers were everywhere.** So at one point after I moved to Belfast, Maine, I was really tickled to look out my apartment window and realize there was an elderflower tree right outside in the back alley. It took me only eight months to notice it! By then it was June, so I kept my eye on that tree, waiting for the blossoms to be just right for harvesting. One morning, I was sitting at my kitchen table when I heard this funny noise outside; it turned out to be the sound of buckets hitting the pavement. Everyone else in the neighborhood had this tree pegged, too, and they'd come to get as many blossoms as they could to make jams or—like me—fritters. I cursed every single one of them as I hoisted myself up to the very top of the tree to get the only flowers left, the ones the early birds had left behind after picking clean the low-hanging branches.

Elderflower has this soft, subtle floral flavor that's got just the tiniest bit of earthiness to it. In the summer I love making this treat—which, though sophisticated-sounding, is really just a good old-fashioned, trashy-in-all-the-right-ways doughboy.

**SERVES 6**

# Elderflower Fritters

Heat oil in a deep fryer to 375°F or, alternatively, heat 2 inches of oil in a heavy-bottomed pan to the same temperature. (You can test if the oil is ready by dropping a small blob of batter into it; the batter should bubble and then brown within 30 to 40 seconds.)

Check the elderflowers for bugs (you're working with nature here!). Trim the stems to ½ inch, then gently rinse the flowers and dry them on paper towels.

Make the batter by combining the flour, sugar, salt, and lemon zest in a medium bowl. Whisk as you slowly add the sparkling water and continue whisking until the batter is completely smooth.

Vegetable oil, for frying

12 to 18 elderflower blossoms

1 cup all-purpose flour

¼ cup confectioners' sugar, plus more for serving

¼ teaspoon salt

Grated zest of 1 lemon

1½ cups sparkling water

Dip each elderflower blossom into the batter. Gently shake off any excess and drop into the hot oil, cooking 4 to 6 at a time. Do not overcrowd the oil or the temperature will drop and the fritters' coating will get soggy. Fry, turning as needed, until the fritters are golden brown, 2 to 4 minutes. Remove the fritters with a slotted spoon and transfer to paper towels to blot any excess grease. Dust with confectioners' sugar and serve warm.

# ELDERFLOWER CORDIAL

If you're going to go to the trouble of tracking down elderflowers—or manage to have a secret stash all your own—I highly recommend making this sweet drink to enjoy as an aperitif, after-dinner libation, or treat on a hot summer day. This cordial is non-alcoholic by nature, but hey, feel free to add a splash (or three) of Prosecco. Add two tablespoons of the cordial to a glass of sparkling water or wine and enjoy. This recipe would also be delicious made with herbs like thyme or rosemary, or other flowers such as violets in place of the elderflowers.

MAKES ABOUT 3 CUPS

2 cups sugar

12 elderflower blossoms, stemmed

Grated zest and juice of 1 lemon

½ tablespoon citric acid

In a medium saucepan, combine 2 cups water with the sugar. Bring it to a boil, then remove the pan from the heat and let the syrup cool to room temperature. Add the elderflowers, lemon zest and juice, and citric acid and stir to combine. Cover the pan and leave it at room temperature for 2 days to infuse.

Strain the cordial through a fine-mesh sieve into jars (discard the elderflowers) and refrigerate for up to 2 weeks or freeze to keep longer.

**There's a brief moment in summer,** smack-dab in the middle of the season, when you can get all these berries at once: strawberries, raspberries, blackberries, and blueberries. And when that happens, you don't mess with their magical perfection. I love them heaped on these scone-like shortcakes with some fresh whipped cream, but in a pinch, skip the shortcakes and enjoy the berries and cream by the bowlful.

**SERVES 8**

# Summer Berries
## WITH GINGER-CREAM SHORTCAKES

Preheat the oven to 375°F. Line a baking sheet with parchment.

**MAKE THE SHORTCAKES:** In a food processor, combine the flour, granulated sugar, baking powder, and lemon zest. Add the butter and pulse until the butter is incorporated and the mixture resembles a coarse meal. Transfer to a large bowl. Using a wooden spoon, mix in the candied ginger, vanilla, and ¾ cup of the heavy cream until just barely combined.

Turn the dough onto a lightly floured surface and form it into a log about 10 inches long and 2 inches wide. Using a knife, slice the dough into 8 circles and put them on the lined baking sheet. Brush the shortcakes with the remaining ¼ cup cream and sprinkle with the raw sugar.

Bake until the shortcakes are light golden, 15 to 18 minutes. Allow them to cool on the baking sheet, then halve them horizontally as though opening a biscuit and divide the bottoms among 8 plates.

**FOR THE SHORTCAKES**

2¼ cups all-purpose flour, plus more for shaping the dough

⅓ cup granulated sugar

1 tablespoon baking powder

Grated zest of 1 lemon

12 tablespoons (1½ sticks) unsalted butter, cold, cut into tablespoon-sized pieces

⅓ cup chopped candied ginger

2 teaspoons vanilla extract

1 cup heavy cream

¼ cup raw sugar

1 pint heavy cream

2 teaspoons vanilla
extract

1 tablespoon
confectioners' sugar,
plus more for serving

½ pint strawberries,
sliced

½ pint raspberries

½ pint blueberries

½ pint blackberries

Mint sprigs, for garnish
(optional)

While the shortcakes bake, make the filling: Using a whisk, hand mixer, or stand mixer fitted with the whisk attachment, whip the cream until soft peaks form. Add the vanilla and confectioners' sugar and mix until just combined.

Spoon a heaping dollop of whipped cream over the bottom half of each scone. Top with a mixture of the berries and another dollop of cream. Top with the other half of the shortcakes, then sprinkle with confectioners' sugar, garnish with mint sprigs, if desired, and serve.

**This recipe was born from a total screw-up.** My plan was to make basil ice cream, but about fifteen minutes before people walked in my door for dinner, I realized I wasn't going to have time to freeze it. Panic set in, so I just folded the custard base into whipped cream and made a lovely, delicious, fluffy, mousse-like custard cream instead. The only thing that improves it is a big bowl of fresh blueberries.

SERVES 8

# Fresh Blueberries
## WITH BASIL CUSTARD CREAM

1 cup whole milk

3 cups heavy cream

¼ cup sugar

1 cup basil leaves, plus more for garnish

4 large egg yolks

1 pint blueberries

In a small saucepan, combine the milk, 1 cup of the cream, and the sugar. Bring to a slow boil over low heat, just to let the sugar dissolve. Remove from the heat.

Tear the basil leaves and add them to the hot mixture. Let steep for 20 minutes.

Meanwhile, whisk the egg yolks in a small bowl. Slowly pour the cream mixture into the yolks, whisking constantly until well incorporated. Return the mixture to the saucepan and cook over medium-high heat, whisking constantly, until the mixture thickens slightly but does not boil. Strain it through a fine-mesh sieve and discard the basil and any curdled egg bits. Transfer to the refrigerator and chill completely.

Whip the remaining 2 cups cream to stiff peaks. Fold in the custard and serve in bowls with the blueberries, garnishing with basil leaves.

**My grandpa Jack—or Gramps,** as we sometimes called him—was a fixture at my dad's diner, always on the line, whistling, flipping eggs. He made the mashed potatoes and was the prime rib master. People still talk about Jack's recipe for the "au jus" sauce. He was also the one to make the dumplings, and he swore by this magical all-purpose baking mix where you just had to add water to make anything—biscuits, pancakes, *anything*. I've yet to figure out his exact recipe, but in my tinkering I discovered this supersimple biscuit recipe to sit atop a cobbler—this one featuring peaches laced with spicy-sweet candied ginger. Pair it with whipped cream or ice cream—or both!

**SERVES 6**

# Peach & Ginger Cobbler

Preheat the oven to 425°F.

**MAKE THE FILLING:** Slice the peaches into wedges and toss them in a medium bowl with the ginger, granulated sugar, lemon zest and juice, and cornstarch until well coated. Let the mixture sit for 20 minutes.

**MEANWHILE, MAKE THE TOPPING:** In a medium bowl, whisk together the flour, granulated sugar, baking powder, salt, and zest. Using a pastry blender, fork, or your fingers, work in the butter until it's in pea-sized pieces. Stir in the candied ginger, then the buttermilk. If the mixture seems too dry to spoon over the fruit, add a bit more buttermilk.

Pour the peaches into a 12-inch ovenproof skillet, preferably cast iron, or a 9 × 13-inch baking dish or porcelain pie dish.

Drop 8 biscuit-sized dollops of the mixture on top of the peaches. Sprinkle with raw sugar and bake until the peaches are tender and bubbly and the topping is golden and cooked through, 25 to 30 minutes. Serve warm.

**FOR THE FILLING**

6 ripe but firm peaches

1 tablespoon grated fresh ginger

¼ cup granulated sugar

Grated zest and juice of 1 lemon

1 teaspoon cornstarch

**FOR THE TOPPING**

1 cup all-purpose flour

½ cup granulated sugar

1 teaspoon baking powder

½ teaspoon salt

2 teaspoons grated lemon zest

6 tablespoons (¾ stick) unsalted butter, cold, cubed

¼ cup chopped candied ginger

⅓ cup buttermilk, or more if needed

Raw sugar

If the only cantaloupe you've had is that sad, anemic proxy in bad fruit salads, then I'd argue you haven't really had it at all. When this melon is perfectly fresh and ripe, it is luscious, syrupy, and richly perfumed. It's absolutely perfect as is, perhaps bettered only as a vehicle for my take on an after-dinner cordial.

**SERVES 8**

2 cups ruby port

1 small cantaloupe

Mint sprigs, for garnish

# Ripe Cantaloupe & Ruby Port Ice

Freeze the port in an ice cream maker until icy and frozen, 15 to 20 minutes. If you don't have an ice cream machine, you can pour the port into a shallow dish or baking pan and freeze completely, then use a fork to scrape the port into flakes. Store in the freezer, covered, for up to a month.

Halve and seed the melon and slice it into 8 wedges. Remove the port ice from the freezer and put a good-sized scoop on top of each melon wedge. Garnish with mint and serve immediately.

## Summer's End

In September, I always look back on how terribly short the summer was, wondering why it can't last longer, and thinking about all the extra time I needed to accomplish everything that I had hoped to do and somehow never got to. I think about the solemn promises I made to dry bunches and bunches of lavender or take that camping trip to Swan's Island—neither of which I ever manage to fit in. It's easy to contemplate all that we *didn't* do, see, or make. Instead, whenever I feel frustrated, robbed of time, in desperate need of more of this season I love so much, I try to take a moment to remember all that I *did* do, all that I *did* see, and all that I *did* make.

While rummaging through old journals, I found this list from a couple summers ago:

- Used a table saw for the first time.

- Built 8 tables from reclaimed boards from a neighbor's barn. I've still got the splinters to prove it.

- Gutted a 1965 Airstream with a sledgehammer and my bare hands and turned it into a kitchen. Hosted a slew of pop-up suppers.

- Adopted a dog. Still questioning who rescued whom.

- Hitched up and trailered a 24-foot camper solo (well, the dog was with me).

- Stopped at every flea market I came across. Got a birdcage, vintage Limoges, and a retro juicer, to name a few treasures. Discovered my unknown talent for dickering.

- Foraged for wild peas, mustard greens, strawberries, blueberries, blackberries, and sea heather. Got poison ivy twice.

- Took up yoga. Finally.

- Cooked with rose hips for the first time ever. Not for the last time.

- Made it my mission to find the best burger in Maine. Hands-down winner, Owls Head General Store.

- Got a wicked suntan. Years overdue.

- Rediscovered vinyl. Life's better with the crackle of Billie Holiday in the background.

- Ate popovers slathered in butter to my heart's content overlooking Jordan Pond at Acadia National Park.

- Learned the art of building a fire. And how to pick a perfect "nighttime log" . . . after many frigid early summer mornings in my cabin.

- Took the ferry to Vinalhaven just to eat ice cream and lie on the beach. Twice.

- Swam in the ocean on a hot day. First time in years. Never felt so relaxed.

- Had a picnic in a greenhouse in the pouring rain.

- Cooked barefoot under an apple orchard, by candlelight.

- Ate more than my fair share of s'mores.

- Stopped to take in the smells of the salty ocean breezes, fresh cut fields of hay, and of course . . . the roses.

# COCKTAIL BREAK

———

Just before opening the Lost Kitchen, I discovered that there are rare liquor laws in effect in Freedom that date back to Prohibition. Prohibition? In *Freedom*? Ironic, I know. It turns out that Maine was actually the instigator of laws in 1846 that prohibited the sale of spirits for any reason other than medical purposes. Once Prohibition ended in 1933, the laws remained intact in Maine, unless each individual town made an effort to vote and overturn them. It wasn't that Freedom couldn't be swayed to update these mandates—there just never was a need in this tiny town; there weren't any shops or restaurants. Eventually a general store opened and overturned the provisions relating to the retail sale of alcohol. The Lost Kitchen was the first establishment to need a license to pour and sell a glass of wine.

I could have gone through the rigors of changing the laws. I even pulled all of the paperwork and began collecting signatures to take the matter to a vote. But then I decided to stay rogue—just like the roots of my supper club. I found a loophole in the existing laws and ended up carving out a wine shop in the foundation of the mill where guests could buy a bottle to accompany their meal. We called it, fittingly, Foundation Wine Cellar. We threw together shelves made from old barn timbers and used flea market–find enamel buckets and ice boxes to chill bottles of rosé and Prosecco for the grabbing.

It turned out to be outrageously beautiful. I think it is so special how guests have to search out the small stone path leading to a side door in the cellar to discover our tucked-away collection of booze, each bottle wrapped in a brown paper bag and tied up with baker's twine. I love the informality of guests bringing their own libations into the restaurant, too; it's as though they've come to my home for supper and are making their contribution to the evening.

I know how much I enjoy showing up to someone else's home, a bottle of spirits tucked under an arm and a cocktail in mind—either based on an infused simple syrup or simply a bottle of ginger beer. All the cocktail recipes here make charming bedfellows with seasonal dishes and are just simple enough to transport with ease.

## SPRING

Rhubarb Gin Fizz
Maple Manhattan

## SUMMER

Sea Rose & Cucumber Gin and Tonic
Blackberry Basil Mojito

## FALL

Spicy Cider & Cilantro Margarita
Cider-Prosecco Cocktail

## WINTER

Dark & Very Stormy
Honeyed Hot Toddy with Thyme

# Rhubarb Gin Fizz

**MAKES 1 COCKTAIL**

2 cups chopped rhubarb

1 cup sugar

1 ounce gin

1 egg white

1 ounce fresh lemon juice

½ ounce half-and-half

4 drops rose water

Ice

Sparkling water

Combine the rhubarb, sugar, and 1 cup water in a saucepan. Bring to a boil, then reduce the heat so that the water simmers, and cook until the rhubarb is softened, 5 to 8 minutes. Cool to room temperature and strain through a fine-mesh sieve.

Combine 1 ounce of the rhubarb simple syrup, the gin, egg white, lemon juice, and half-and-half in a cocktail shaker. Shake vigorously for 30 seconds, then add ice and shake for another 30 seconds. Strain the mixture into a coupe or highball glass and top with a splash of sparkling water. Save the leftover rhubarb simple syrup in the fridge for up to a month.

# Maple Manhattan

**MAKES 1 COCKTAIL**

2 ounces rye whiskey

½ ounce sweet vermouth

½ ounce maple syrup

2 dashes of Angostura bitters

Ice

Maraschino cherry, for garnish (or liquor-soaked fresh cherries, if you can find them)

Combine the whiskey, vermouth, maple syrup, and bitters in a cocktail shaker filled with ice. Shake for 30 seconds and strain into a chilled martini glass. Garnish with a cherry.

# Sea Rose & Cucumber Gin and Tonic

**MAKES 2 COCKTAILS**

1 seedless cucumber, halved

Ice

4 ounces good gin, such as Hendrick's

Good tonic water, such as Q

1 teaspoon rose water

2 teaspoons fresh lime juice

Rose petals, preferably from organic sea roses, for garnish

1 baby cucumber, sliced lengthwise into ¼-inch spears, for garnish (optional)

Start by juicing the seedless cucumber. If you don't have a juicer, use a blender or food processor to puree it completely, then strain the juice through a fine-mesh sieve.

Fill 2 highball glasses with ice. Add ½ ounce cucumber juice to each glass. Add 2 ounces gin to each and top with tonic water. Finish each glass with ½ teaspoon rose water and 1 teaspoon lime juice. Give a stir and garnish with a rose petal and a slice of baby cucumber. Cheers!

# Blackberry Basil Mojito

**MAKES 1 COCKTAIL**

¼ cup blackberries

10 basil leaves, torn

2 tablespoons superfine sugar

½ lime, cut into 4 pieces

Ice

2 ounces light rum

Sparkling water

Put the blackberries in a tumbler and muddle or crush with a wooden spoon. Strain the juice through a fine-mesh sieve into a small bowl. Give the tumbler a quick rinse to remove any berry seeds.

Combine the blackberry juice, basil, sugar, and lime and muddle again.

Fill a tall glass with ice. Pour in the blackberry mixture (don't strain it) and add the rum and a splash of sparkling water. Give everything a stir and serve.

## Spicy Cider & Cilantro Margarita

**MAKES 1 COCKTAIL**

Kosher salt

½ ounce fresh lime juice, plus more for rim

Ice

2 ounces tequila

½ ounce orange liqueur, such as Cointreau or Triple Sec

1 ounce apple cider

½ ounce Cilantro Simple Syrup (page 73)

Lime wedge

Put some salt in a shallow bowl. Rub the rim of a highball glass with lime juice and then dip it into the salt to coat.

Fill a cocktail shaker with ice. Add the tequila, orange liqueur, cider, cilantro simple syrup, and lime juice and shake for 30 seconds. Fill a glass with ice and strain the cocktail into the glass. Garnish with a lime wedge.

## Cider–Prosecco Cocktail

**MAKES 1 COCKTAIL**

½ ounce apple cider, chilled

½ ounce Rosemary Simple Syrup (page 73)

½ ounce Cognac

Prosecco, chilled

Rosemary sprig, for garnish

Pour the apple cider, rosemary simple syrup, and Cognac into a champagne glass. Top with Prosecco and garnish with a sprig of rosemary.

# Dark & Very Stormy

**MAKES 1 COCKTAIL**

Ice

2 ounces dark rum

¼ ounce fresh lime juice

1 (8-ounce) bottle of ginger beer

Rosemary sprig, for garnish

Fill a highball glass with ice. Add the rum and lime juice and then top with ginger beer. Garnish with a rosemary sprig.

# Honeyed Hot Toddy with Thyme

**MAKES 1 COCKTAIL**

2 ounces bourbon

1 tablespoon honey

1 teaspoon fresh lemon juice

1 sprig of fresh thyme

¼ cup boiling water

In a mug or a Mason jar, combine the bourbon, honey, lemon juice, and thyme. Pour in the boiling water and let sit for 30 seconds. Stir and enjoy.

**Infusing Spirits**   One of the easiest ways to dress up vodka is to infuse it with fruit or herbs. Stuff a quart jar full of strawberries, raspberries, lemons, thyme, rosemary, or elderberries (to name just a few possibilities) and fill it with vodka. No need for Grey Goose (though also not an excuse for a bargain brand); I like Absolut. If the flavoring you've chosen is normally very tart or unsweet, add ¾ to 1 cup sugar. Give the jar a turn once a day—or when you think of it—and let sit for two to three weeks if infusing something more fragile like strawberries, or up to a month for tougher elderberries or rosemary. As long as the fruit or herbs are covered, there's no need to refrigerate it. Enjoy straight up or mixed into other cocktails.

# FALL

———

## LEAVES, TWIGS & ROOTS

I crave warmth in autumn. Whether it takes the form of a sun-drenched fall day (when the trees explode in brilliant hues of crimson and citrine) or a first-of-the-season fire, it's like a last warm hurrah of sorts before all becomes stark and cold until spring. Soon the trees will be bare, the landscape grayed from the first frost, and the daylight will dwindle . . . not to mention I'll have to rake up all of those damn leaves! But it's the thought of the comforting dishes of the season that brings me back to this lovely moment between two worlds, no longer warm, and yet not so cold. Come autumn I crave rich, slow-cooked meats, creamy wedges of roasted squash, hearty stews, and swigs of sweet apple cider. This is the season that calls for dishes that leave us feeling full and loved.

# FIRSTS

Nibbles for Hot Toddies
  *Crispy Parsnip Ribbons*
  *Warmed Olives*
Sunchoke Soup with Crème Fraîche & Marigolds
Waldorf Salad with Apple, Fennel & Candied Walnuts
Warm Mushroom Toast with Port, Herbs & Ricotta
Roasted Buttercup Squash Cups with Apple Slaw
Sweet & Sour Apple Cider Chicken Wings with Cilantro

# MAINS

Fried Rabbit with Charred Radicchio & Mustard Vinaigrette
Rosemary-Brined Pork Chops with Apples, Potatoes & Brandy
Slow-Roasted Pork Picnic Shoulder with Cinnamon & Rosemary
Apple Cider–Glazed Duck
A Stew of Moose with Parsley Dumplings

# SWEETS

Rustic Plum & Honey Pie with Vanilla Bean Soured Cream
Apple Cider Doughnuts
Sweet Nutmeg Custard
Caramelized Pear & Cornmeal Skillet Cake
Spiced Squash Chiffon Pie

# Nibbles for Hot Toddies

These are requisite snacks for huddling around a wood fire, mugs in hand. See page 147 for my favorite hot toddy recipe.

## CRISPY PARSNIP RIBBONS

I love putting these out in a little vintage bowl because they're long and curly and almost nest-like when tufted together. They're also lovely alongside soups.

**SERVES 4 TO 6**

Vegetable oil, for frying

1 large parsnip

Salt

Heat oil in a deep fryer to 375°F or, alternatively, heat 2 inches of oil in a heavy-bottomed pan to the same temperature.

Using a vegetable peeler or mandoline, slice the parsnip lengthwise in long, thin ribbons.

Drop a handful of the ribbons into the hot oil and fry until golden, 15 to 20 seconds. Remove the ribbons with tongs or a slotted spoon and blot on paper towels. Toss them to "fluff" and sprinkle with salt.

# WARMED OLIVES

Warmed olives are not only comforting but also a bit unexpected. Warming the olives ever so slightly intensifies their flavor. This recipe offers just one suggestion for aromatics you can use. Also delicious would be garlic cloves, grapefruit or clementine peels, and any hearty herbs.

Make sure to buy olives that are packed in brine, as you'll want to reserve the brine for storing the prepared olives.

**MAKES 2 CUPS**

2 cups mixed olives with pits

1 cup olive oil

Needles from 1 rosemary sprig

Leaves from 2 thyme sprigs

2 bay leaves

Zest of 1 orange, removed with a vegetable peeler

Combine the ingredients in a small saucepan and heat over low heat until warm. Transfer to a bowl and serve, leaving the bay leaves and zest as garnish.

**Often what I cook** depends on who shows up at my restaurant's back door. I first got my hands on sunchokes when a farmer turned up with a five-pound pickle tub of them, freshly dug and still cold from the earth. At first glance, they didn't look like much—all knobbly and caked with mud and stones. I painstakingly scrubbed away the dirt (a task that grocery stores and farmer's market booths will have taken care of for you!), cooked them to creamy tenderness, and pureed them into this soup. I couldn't believe the transformation from dirty and rugged to velvety and refined. Their earthy nuttiness makes for a rich dish, rendered even more decadent by tangy crème fraîche and surprisingly robust marigolds. I can still smell my mother's garden when I sprinkle the flower leaves over the bowl. Not to worry; if you don't have marigolds growing at home, this soup would be just as tasty with a small sprinkling of herbs, such as mint, marjoram, thyme, or chives, or even their blossoms.

This recipe calls for a fine-mesh sieve. I don't have a ton of cooking supplies, but this is an essential for me. While your soup will still be delicious without being strained, the lovely silkiness that comes from passing it through a sieve is unparalleled.

SERVES 4

# Sunchoke Soup
## WITH CRÈME FRAÎCHE & MARIGOLDS

¼ cup olive oil

1 pound white, yellow, or sweet onions, sliced thin

Salt and pepper

2 pounds sunchokes, peeled

1 garlic clove

2 bay leaves

4 sprigs of fresh thyme

4 tablespoons (½ stick) unsalted butter

1½ cups half-and-half

1 cup heavy cream

½ teaspoon grated nutmeg

¼ cup crème fraîche

Marigold petals, for garnish (optional)

Dill fronds, for garnish

Heat 2 tablespoons of the olive oil in a large skillet, preferably cast iron, over medium-low heat, toss in the onions and a sprinkle of salt, and cook over low heat, stirring occasionally, until the onions are deeply caramelized, 30 to 45 minutes.

Meanwhile, put the sunchokes in a 4-quart pot, cover with cold water, and add the garlic, bay leaves, thyme, and 2 tablespoons salt. Bring to a boil over high heat, then reduce the heat and simmer the sunchokes until tender and easily pierced with a fork, 12 to 15 minutes.

Drain the sunchokes, discarding the aromatics, and add to the onions. Puree the sunchokes and onions in a blender, working in batches if needed, while still hot. Add the butter, remaining 2 tablespoons olive oil, the half-and-half, cream, and nutmeg and season with salt and pepper to taste. Pulse to blend.

Strain the soup through a fine-mesh sieve into a medium pot. Reheat gently without boiling. Ladle the soup into 4 shallow bowls and top each with a dollop of crème fraîche and a sprinkling of marigold petals, if using, and dill fronds.

**My mom would make a version** of this classic salad all the time when I was growing up, often to accompany baked beans and "red snappy" hot dogs as a sneaky way to get in some fruits and veggies. I still love the combination of flavors, but now I like to up the ante with fennel and candied walnuts, which are sweet and salty in all the right ways.

SERVES 4

# Waldorf Salad
## WITH APPLES, FENNEL & CANDIED WALNUTS

In a large bowl, combine the apples, fennel, celery, and lemon zest and juice. Toss to coat. Add the walnuts, mayo, and parsley and toss again. Season to taste with salt and pepper.

Make a bed of radicchio on individual plates or a platter, top with the dressed mixture, and garnish with fennel fronds and celery leaves.

2 crisp apples, cut into ½-inch cubes

1 small fennel bulb, cored and sliced, fronds reserved for garnish

2 celery stalks, sliced, leaves reserved for garnish

Grated zest and juice of ½ lemon

½ cup candied walnuts (see page 77)

⅓ cup mayonnaise, homemade (page 37) or store-bought

¼ cup fresh parsley leaves

Salt and pepper

1 heaping handful of radicchio, or good-looking greens such as Bibb lettuce or arugula

When you work with foragers, you never know when they're going to show up, what they're going to bring, and how much. Sometimes they come in on the verge of tears, complaining that there's been no rain. And sometimes they come in with truckloads—and there's no way you can pass it all up so you've got to think on your feet to use everything. This dish came about when one of my mushroom guys turned up with baskets and baskets of different types of mushrooms. I thought back to one of my favorite ways to eat them: buttered and sautéed in port, reminiscent of my dad's campfire version from our days camping up at Mount Katahdin. Then I spooned them over a schmear of ricotta cheese on toasted sourdough, and layered in the damp, mossy taste of the woods with a whisper of thyme and rosemary.

SERVES 4

# Warm Mushroom Toast
## WITH PORT, HERBS & RICOTTA

2 tablespoons olive oil, plus more for drizzling

½ pound mixed mushrooms, such as cremini, shiitake, and button

2 sprigs of fresh thyme

1 sprig of fresh rosemary

Salt and pepper

¼ cup port

3 tablespoons unsalted butter

4 thick slices of good sourdough bread

1 garlic clove

½ cup ricotta

Small handful of arugula

¼ cup pecorino shavings

Preheat the oven to 425°F.

Set a large ovenproof skillet, preferably cast iron, over high heat and pour in the olive oil. Add the mushrooms, thyme, and rosemary. Season with a good pinch of salt and a few twists of pepper. Sauté for 1 minute.

Add the port and bring to a boil. Cook for a minute, then add the butter and transfer the pan to the oven. Roast until the mushrooms are just tender, 5 minutes.

Meanwhile, drizzle the bread with a little olive oil and crisp it up in the oven (or on a hot grill or in a toaster). When just golden and crisp, about 4 minutes, rub the toast with the garlic clove.

Top each piece of bread with a schmear of ricotta, a few leaves of arugula, and mushrooms and a bit of pan juice. Sprinkle with pecorino and serve. Yum.

My parents would always make squash the same way: half-moon pieces, a pinch of salt, a sprinkle of nutmeg, and a knob of butter, swaddled in foil and roasted in the oven or nestled among the coals on the grill. It's such a fond food memory for me that I wanted to find a way to combine it with some other fall flavors. Wedges of buttercup squash make the perfect shape for cradling a salad of arugula and crisp apple slaw.

SERVES 4

# Roasted Buttercup Squash Cups
## WITH APPLE SLAW

1 small buttercup squash (about 2½ pounds), cut into 4 wedges and seeded

½ cup olive oil

Salt and pepper

1 teaspoon grated nutmeg

4 tablespoons (½ stick) unsalted butter

1 small shallot, finely diced

2 tablespoons seasoned rice wine vinegar

2 crisp apples

1 tablespoon maple syrup

1 tablespoon fresh thyme leaves

1 small handful of arugula

Preheat the oven to 425°F.

Brush the squash flesh with ¼ cup of the olive oil and season each piece with 1 teaspoon salt, a few twists of black pepper, and ¼ teaspoon nutmeg. Top each with a tablespoon of butter, wrap individually in foil, and bake until the squash is fork-tender, 25 to 30 minutes.

Combine the shallot and rice wine vinegar in a small bowl and allow to macerate as you make the apple slaw.

Slice the apples into matchsticks using the matchstick blade on a mandoline or a knife. Toss the apple with the shallots and vinegar along with the maple syrup, remaining ¼ cup olive oil, and the thyme. Taste and season with salt and pepper.

To serve, put a small bed of arugula in the valley of each warm squash wedge and top with a handful of apple slaw.

**I have a major soft spot for chicken wings.** Give me a margarita and some buffalo wings and I'm a very, very happy girl. To elevate my favorite food and make it something I can be proud to serve in a vintage bowl, I created my own secret sauce, kind of a fancy version of McDonald's sweet and sour (which, if you're like me, you hate to admit that you love on rare occasions).

**SERVES 6 TO 8**

# Sweet & Sour Apple Cider Chicken Wings with Cilantro

2 to 3 pounds chicken wings

Basic Brine (page 170)

½ cup apple cider

3 tablespoons apple cider vinegar

¼ cup packed light brown sugar

1 tablespoon ketchup

2 teaspoons cornstarch

¼ teaspoon salt

½ cup fresh cilantro leaves

1 lime, cut into 6 to 8 pieces

In a non-reactive dish big enough to hold the chicken and brine, submerge the chicken wings, cover, and refrigerate for 24 to 36 hours.

In a small saucepan, combine the apple cider, vinegar, brown sugar, ketchup, cornstarch, and salt. Bring to a boil and whisk over medium-high heat until the mixture thickens, about 5 minutes.

Drain the chicken wings. You can either fry or roast them.

**TO FRY:** Heat oil in a deep fryer to 375°F or, alternatively, heat 2 inches of oil in a heavy-bottomed pan to the same temperature.

Working in batches of 5 to 8 wings so the oil temperature doesn't drop, fry the wings, turning once, until golden, 4 to 5 minutes. Drain on paper towels and toss with the sauce.

**TO ROAST:** Preheat the oven to 425°F.

Toss the wings in half of the sauce, arrange the wings on a baking sheet, and roast until golden and crispy, 15 to 20 minutes. Toss the wings with the remaining sauce.

Sprinkle the sauced wings with the cilantro and serve hot with the lime wedges.

When I started the restaurant, I had no idea how to cook rabbit. But there I was with some rabbits courtesy of my poultry guy, so I went to my foolproof cooking method for rich meats: confit. I rubbed the pieces in salt and spices, let them cure overnight, and then slowly cooked them in fat. The result was wonderfully rich—perfect for a salad of bitter radicchio (I can just see rabbits munching on those leaves after all the more delicate ones have wilted from the frost), bits of sweet pear, and a sharp mustard vinaigrette for zing. You need only a glass of rosé to round out this hearty lunch or indulgent main course.

I strongly urge you to seek out rabbit. Don't be scared! But should courage or availability fail you, duck legs would suit just fine.

SERVES 4

# Fried Rabbit
## WITH CHARRED RADICCHIO & MUSTARD VINAIGRETTE

**FOR THE CONFIT**

4 rabbit legs (or
4 duck legs)

2 tablespoons roughly
chopped fresh rosemary

1 tablespoon fresh
thyme leaves

2 large garlic cloves,
sliced

1 large shallot, sliced

2 tablespoons kosher
salt

4 cups rendered duck
fat, melted

**START THE CONFIT:** In a medium bowl, combine the rabbit legs, rosemary, thyme, garlic, shallot, and salt. Cover and refrigerate for 24 hours to cure.

Preheat the oven to 250°F.

Gently brush the cure mixture from the rabbit. Put the legs in a small baking dish—just large enough to accommodate them in a single layer—and pour in duck fat until they are completely submerged. Transfer the dish to the oven and cook until the rabbit is lightly browned and tender, about 4 hours. The meat should be falling off the bone. Remove from the oven and allow the rabbit to come to room temperature in the duck fat.

*(recipe continues)*

**MEANWHILE, MAKE THE VINAIGRETTE:** Combine the shallot and vinegar in a small bowl and let macerate for 15 minutes. Whisk in the mustard, then keep whisking as you slowly pour in the olive oil. Add the thyme and pepper to taste.

Heat oil in a deep fryer to 375°F or, alternatively, heat 2 inches of oil in a heavy-bottomed pan to the same temperature.

While the oil heats, set a large cast-iron skillet, sauté pan, or grill pan over medium-high heat. Brush the radicchio wedges with olive oil. Sear the radicchio in the hot pan until the leaves brown, 1 to 2 minutes. Repeat on the other cut side.

Meanwhile, remove the rabbit legs from the rendered fat and fry until golden brown and warmed through, 3 to 4 minutes. Divide the radicchio wedges among 4 plates and arrange the pear slices alongside. Lay the legs beside the radicchio and drizzle the radicchio and pears with mustard vinaigrette. Garnish each plate with a sprig of thyme, if desired.

### FOR THE VINAIGRETTE

1 small shallot, diced

2 tablespoons seasoned rice wine vinegar

1 tablespoon Dijon mustard

¼ cup olive oil

1 teaspoon fresh thyme leaves

Pepper

Vegetable oil, for frying

1 large head radicchio, quartered

Olive oil

2 small ripe pears, sliced

4 sprigs of thyme, for garnish (optional)

There comes a time in November when you realize you can't just grab a jacket and head out the door to take the dog for a walk; you have to adorn yourself in blaze orange so as not to be mistaken for deer. Right before Thanksgiving for four to six weeks, six days a week (there's no hunting on Sundays), people are out looking for game to fill their freezers for winter. You can't go to the general store without coming across a truck strapped with someone's deer, and neighbors come knocking on each other's doors to share their bounty (there's only so much venison one can eat all winter). This dish is inspired by my favorite way to cook venison, but uses pork instead—which is most likely much easier to come by in your neck of the woods. It also represents all the flavors that I smell in the air come hunting season.

**SERVES 4**

# Rosemary-Brined Pork Chops
## WITH APPLES, POTATOES & BRANDY

Basic Brine (page 170) made with 4 rosemary sprigs

4 bone-in pork chops (each about 1½ inches thick)

1 pound baby potatoes

Salt and pepper

6 tablespoons olive oil

4 tablespoons (½ stick) unsalted butter

2 sprigs of rosemary, needles finely chopped

2 large shallots, sliced lengthwise

2 crisp apples, peeled, quartered, and cored

¼ cup Calvados or other good apple brandy

Submerge the pork chops in the cooled brine, cover, and refrigerate for at least 24 and up to 36 hours.

When you're ready to cook the chops, preheat the oven to 425°F.

Put the potatoes in a medium pot and add just enough cold water to cover. Season with salt and bring to a boil, then reduce the heat and simmer the potatoes until just fork-tender, 15 to 20 minutes.

Meanwhile, in a small skillet, preferably cast iron, over medium-high heat, combine 2 tablespoons of the olive oil, 2 tablespoons of the butter, and the chopped rosemary. Once the butter has melted, add the shallots and cook until softened, 8 to 10 minutes. Add the apples and cook for 5 minutes, stirring occasionally.

*(recipe continues)*

Add the Calvados, stir, and cook for another minute. Reduce the heat to low, add the remaining 2 tablespoons butter, and cook until the apples are just tender, about 5 more minutes. Drain the potatoes and toss with the apple mixture.

Heat 2 large ovenproof skillets, preferably cast iron (or work in batches in one pan), over high heat with 2 tablespoons of the olive oil in each. Remove the pork chops from the brine and pat dry with paper towels. When the oil shimmers, carefully add the chops to the pans and sear until golden, about 2 minutes. Flip and cook for another 2 minutes. Transfer the pans to the oven and roast until the pork is cooked to your liking—I prefer medium, which will register as 140°F to 145°F on a meat thermometer. Depending on how thick your chops are, this could take 5 to 10 minutes. Allow the chops to rest on a warm plate for 5 minutes before serving.

Serve the pork chops with the warm potatoes and apples.

## BASIC BRINE

Brining seasons your meat from the inside out. It lends flavor and juiciness and is an insurance policy if you're still getting the feel for salt and pepper and/or are nervous about cooking lean cuts of meat without drying them out. It might seem like more work to prepare a brine and soak your meat (for at least 24 and up to 36 hours) in advance of cooking, but it pays dividends in the pan and on the plate. And I assure you that once you've done this once or twice, it won't take you more than 5 minutes of active prep time.

Combine 4 cups water, the salt, sugar, juniper berries, peppercorns, and bay leaves in a pot and bring to a boil. Stir until the salt and sugar dissolve, then remove from the heat and allow to cool completely before using. It will keep in the fridge for up to 2 weeks.

MAKES 4 CUPS, OR
ENOUGH FOR ABOUT
5 POUNDS OF MEAT

⅓ cup kosher salt

⅓ cup sugar

¼ cup juniper berries

2 tablespoons black peppercorns

4 bay leaves

**Fall is a time for roasting.** Having the oven on all day adds welcome warmth to the newly chilled air, and as we slow down for the coming winter, languid, low-maintenance cooking suits the mood. This dish calls for very little in the way of prep. Simply slather the pork with herbs and spices, let it marinate overnight, and then gently roast it for hours as you go about your day.

**SERVES 4 TO 6**

2 tablespoons chopped fresh rosemary

1 tablespoon chopped garlic

1½ tablespoons ground cinnamon

1 tablespoon kosher salt

1 teaspoon cracked pepper

1 boneless pork picnic shoulder (about 3 pounds)

2 tablespoons olive oil

# Slow-Roasted Pork Picnic
## SHOULDER WITH CINNAMON & ROSEMARY

In a small bowl, combine the rosemary, garlic, cinnamon, salt, and pepper.

Slather the pork shoulder with the oil and rub the spices into the meat. Put in a baking dish, cover with plastic wrap, and refrigerate overnight.

Take the pork shoulder out of the fridge 30 minutes before roasting. Preheat the oven to 300°F.

Cover the pork with foil and roast for 5 hours.

Remove the foil and roast for another 15 minutes. The pork should be browned and very tender. Remove the pork from the oven and let it rest for 10 minutes before serving.

**Every once in a while** my grandfather would want to take us out for a big, fancy dinner, and when he did, it was almost always for Chinese food. My memories are replete with elegant lacquered ducks, perfumed and succulent. This version is one that arrives at Peking via Maine. Serve alongside Parsnip Puree (page 226), sautéed greens, or, of course, a bowl of rice.

**SERVES 4**

# Apple Cider–Glazed Duck

Preheat the oven to 350°F.

Pour the apple cider into a medium nonreactive saucepan and boil over medium heat until reduced to 1 cup. Add the honey, cider vinegar, mustard, and butter and continue cooking for 5 minutes. Stir in the chili powder, red pepper flakes, and pie spice and remove from the heat. Let the sauce cool to room temperature and then refrigerate for at least an hour or two, until cold. (You can do this the day before.)

Cut the apple into 8 wedges and slice the shallots in half. Season the cavity of the duck with salt and pepper and stuff with the apple pieces, shallots, and sage. Truss the duck (see page 50).

In a large shallow baking dish or ovenproof skillet, preferably cast iron, toss the onions with the olive oil and spread over the bottom of the dish. Nestle the duck on top.

Brush the duck with some of the glaze (it can still be cold) and roast uncovered, basting periodically with more glaze, until the duck is cooked through and a meat thermometer inserted in the leg reads 175°F, about 1½ hours.

Let rest for 20 minutes before serving.

2 cups apple cider

½ cup honey

¼ cup apple cider vinegar

1 tablespoon Dijon mustard

½ tablespoon unsalted butter

½ teaspoon chili powder

¼ teaspoon crushed red pepper flakes

¼ teaspoon apple pie spice

1 crisp apple, preferably local (Fuji and Honeycrisp work year-round)

2 shallots

1 whole duck ( about 4 pounds)

Salt and pepper

1 bunch of sage

3 large onions, sliced

Olive oil

Only in Maine does your neighbor bring you a beautiful moose steak as a "welcome-to-the-neighborhood" gift. Sure enough, that's exactly what my Maine guide neighbor, Debbie, did. I'd never cooked moose before, but then I remembered my mom's incredible beef stew recipe, and simply subbed in moose for beef. It's a traditional affair, with potatoes, carrots, onions, turnips, peas, and one secret ingredient: beer. But you could easily substitute red wine, and of course, use any cut of beef suitable for stewing (rump or chuck steak, for example) if you can't get your hands on moose.

SERVES 8 TO 10

# A Stew of Moose
## WITH PARSLEY DUMPLINGS

In a large bowl, toss the meat with 2 teaspoons salt, ½ teaspoon pepper, and the flour.

Pour the olive oil into a large heavy-bottomed pot or Dutch oven over high heat. When the oil shimmers, add the meat in batches (if too crowded, it will steam rather than brown). Brown the meat on all sides, about 10 minutes, and remove from the pot.

Add the butter, shallots, and bay leaf to the pot and season with a pinch of salt and a few twists of pepper. Add the garlic, oregano, and basil and stir with a wooden spoon to combine. Pour in the beer and scrape the bottom of the pot to remove all the good brown bits.

Add 3 cups water to the pot, bring to a simmer, and add the moose. Cover, reduce the heat to low, and cook until the moose is tender, 1½ to 2 hours.

Prepare the dumpling dough while the stew cooks.

2 pounds moose, cut into 1-inch cubes

Salt and pepper

1 tablespoon all-purpose flour

2 tablespoons olive oil

2 tablespoons unsalted butter

4 shallots, quartered

1 bay leaf

1 garlic clove, chopped

1 tablespoon chopped fresh oregano

2 tablespoons chopped fresh basil

1 (12-ounce) bottle of beer (on the lighter side)

Parsley Dumpling Dough (page176)

2 celery stalks, cut into ½-inch pieces

4 medium carrots, cut into ½-inch pieces

½ pound potatoes, cut into ½-inch pieces

1 cup frozen peas

*(recipe continues)*

Add the celery, carrots, and potatoes to the stew and simmer, uncovered, until just tender, about 10 minutes.

Making sure the stew is at a slow boil, stir in the frozen peas and dollop the dumpling dough in heaping tablespoons on top of the stew. Cover and cook until the dumplings are just cooked through and a sharp knife inserted in the center comes out clean, 4 to 5 minutes. Serve piping hot.

## PARSLEY DUMPLING DOUGH

If you were eating stew at Grandpa Jack's house—beef, chicken, moose—then you were also having his "famous" dumplings. I can still picture his hands covered in gooey biscuity goodness.

Put all the ingredients in a large bowl, combine, and voilà. Boil the dumplings, each roughly 1 heaping tablespoon in size, in either a stew or a pot of simmering water for 4 to 5 minutes, covered, until they're tender and a sharp knife inserted in the middle comes out clean. Serve hot.

MAKES 1 DOZEN
DUMPLINGS

1 cup all-purpose flour

2 teaspoons baking powder

1 teaspoon salt

1 tablespoon unsalted butter, melted

2 teaspoons confectioners' sugar

½ cup whole milk

2 tablespoons chopped fresh parsley

## The Cheese Board: A Forgotten Ritual

I love to offer a cheese board at the restaurant and when cooking for friends at home because it's a way of taking a pause. People can digest, converse, and unwind after a good meal. And loveliest of all, there are few if any rules to abide by, only opportunities to showcase the brilliant cheesemakers in your area:

- **Forget the "one soft, one hard, one blue, one goat, one cow" edict:** Just focus on great cheese. If you find two that day, that'll work. Three? Awesome. And if one happens to be blue and one goat and one cow, then, score, trifecta. But don't try to force it or you may end up passing over a cheese that deserves a spot on your table.

- **No need to buy a fancy marble board:** Look around your house to see what you have. Mismatched plates? Beautiful. An old cutting board you found at the flea market? Perfect. I've even used salvaged slate roof tiles and cedar barn shingles as serving pieces.

- **Pull out the cheese a few hours before serving:** You want cheese at room temperature. If it's hot out, though, make sure it doesn't get sweaty.

- **Give your cheese proper bedfellows:** Candied nuts (see page 77), raw nuts, sliced fresh fruit, dried fruit, pickled fruit, preserves, honey, good crusty bread—whatever inspires.

**I'm not one to fuss over a piecrust;** I lack the patience. In that regard, this recipe speaks to my heart: no fancy latticework, no double crusts, no crimping, and no rules other than don't think about your ex-husband when you're making pastry dough (it'll get tough and overworked). The result is a single, tender crust that's folded free-form over a simple fruit and nut filling. Imperfections welcome!

Feel free to play with this recipe and substitute any fruit you like. Pears, peaches, apples, or berries would all be equally delicious.

# Rustic Plum & Honey Pie
## WITH VANILLA BEAN SOURED CREAM

**SERVES 8**

**MAKE THE PASTRY:** In a food processor, combine the flour, sugar, and salt. Pulse just to combine. Add the butter and water and pulse again until the dough resembles a fluffy cottage cheese. Turn the dough onto a floured surface. With your hands, shape it until it just comes together as a ball. You don't want to overwork the dough or your pastry will get tough. Roll the dough into a 14-inch round, transfer it to a baking sheet, and refrigerate for 30 minutes.

**MIX THE CREAM:** Stir together the sour cream, vanilla extract, and vanilla bean seeds. Set aside.

Preheat the oven to 400°.

**FOR THE PASTRY**

1½ cups all-purpose flour, plus more for rolling the dough

1 tablespoon granulated sugar

½ teaspoon salt

12 tablespoons (1½ sticks) unsalted butter, cold, cut into pieces

⅓ cup ice water

**FOR THE CREAM**

1 cup sour cream

1 teaspoon vanilla extract

½ vanilla bean, split lengthwise and scraped

**PREPARE THE FILLING:** In a small bowl, combine the hazelnuts, ¼ cup of the sugar, and the flour.

Remove the chilled pastry from the refrigerator and spread the nut mixture over the center of the dough, leaving a 2-inch border around the edge. Maintaining the border, lay the plum slices in concentric circles, starting from the outside and working your way to the middle. Fold the border of dough over to cover part of the fruit. Dot the fruit with the butter and sprinkle the entire pie with the remaining ½ cup sugar.

Bake until the fruit is bubbly and the crust is golden brown, about 20 minutes.

While the pie is still warm, drizzle the honey evenly over the fruit to create a glaze.

Once the pie is cool, serve with a dollop of the vanilla bean soured cream.

**FOR THE FILLING**

⅓ cup hazelnuts, toasted and ground

¾ cup granulated sugar

3 tablespoons all-purpose flour

6 plums, cut into ⅛-inch slices

2 tablespoons unsalted butter, cut into pieces

3 tablespoons honey

**One of my earliest food memories** is from when I was in kinder-garten. My dad had just bought the diner, and every morning on our way to school with my mom we'd stop into the restaurant to say good morning. Grandpa Jack would be at the griddle flipping eggs, and my grandmother would be at the fryer making the doughnuts for the day—chocolate, nutmeg, and apple cider. They'd be super-toasty on the outside, soft on the inside, and one of the best things I'd ever tasted.

**MAKES 6 DOUGHNUTS**

# Apple Cider Doughnuts

Boil the cider in a small saucepan over medium heat until reduced to ¾ cup. Set aside to cool.

In a large bowl, whisk together the flour, baking powder, salt, ginger, nutmeg, and ½ teaspoon cinnamon.

In a stand mixer fitted with the paddle attachment or in a large bowl with a wooden spoon, beat together the butter, brown sugar, and ¼ cup of the granulated sugar until light and fluffy. Add the vanilla, egg, and yolk and beat until combined. Slowly add the dry ingredients, alternating with the reduced apple cider. Refrigerate the mixture for 20 to 30 minutes.

Heat oil in a deep fryer to 375°F or, alternatively, heat 2 inches of oil in a heavy-bottomed pan to the same temperature. (You can test if the oil is ready by dropping a small blob of dough into it; the dough should bubble and then brown within 30 to 40 seconds.)

Stir together the remaining 1 cup granulated sugar and 1 tablespoon cinnamon in small bowl.

2 cups apple cider

2 cups all-purpose flour, plus more for rolling the dough

1½ teaspoons baking powder

¼ teaspoon salt

½ teaspoon ground ginger

¼ teaspoon grated nutmeg

1 tablespoon plus ½ teaspoon ground cinnamon

4 tablespoons (½ stick) unsalted butter, at room temperature

½ cup packed light brown sugar

1¼ cups granulated sugar

1 teaspoon vanilla extract

1 large egg

1 large egg yolk

Vegetable oil, for frying

Roll out the dough on a floured surface to 1 inch thick (don't worry; it's supposed to be soft). Cut the doughnuts using a 2½-inch doughnut cutter or two comparable different sizes of biscuit cutters (so you get the rings and the holes).

Working in 2 batches, fry the doughnuts (and holes), flipping continuously, until golden and cooked through, about 4 minutes. Drain on paper towels. Roll the hot doughnuts in the cinnamon sugar and serve.

If I had to think of *the* main dessert my Gram made, it would be custard. It stands to reason: my grandparents were egg farmers at one point, so we were never in short supply. Every Saturday morning it was Grammy eggs: soft-boiled eggs mashed up with butter, salt, and pepper. Then, for dessert, it was custard. In the fall, it would be a simple nutmeg version that was sweet and rich and delicious.

**SERVES 8**

3 cups whole milk

2 teaspoons vanilla extract

1 teaspoon grated nutmeg

⅛ teaspoon ground cinnamon

¼ teaspoon salt

4 large egg yolks

⅓ cup sugar

# Sweet Nutmeg Custard

Preheat the oven to 300°F.

Heat the milk in a saucepan over low heat until just hot. Remove from the heat and add the vanilla, nutmeg, cinnamon, and salt.

In a medium bowl, beat the egg yolks with the sugar, then slowly whisk in the hot milk mixture.

Divide the custard base among eight 6-ounce ramekins and arrange them in a shallow baking dish. Fill the baking dish halfway with hot water and carefully transfer it to the oven. Bake until the custard is set, 45 minutes to 1 hour.

Remove the custard from the water bath, allow to cool to room temperature, and serve. You could also make the custard ahead and refrigerate it (not more than a day in advance). Remove from the fridge 1 hour before serving.

I get a lot of requests to make this cake for special occasions—especially my son's birthday. I think this has to do with how dramatic it is to see the cake flipped from the skillet to reveal the impressive, deeply caramelized amber crown of fanned pear slices. Anyone can pull this off, really. My one recommendation is that you buy good-quality stone-ground cornmeal—not the cheap stuff that tastes like chicken feed.

MAKES 1(12-INCH) CAKE; SERVES 8 TO 10

# Caramelized Pear & Cornmeal Skillet Cake

CARAMELIZE THE PEARS: Peel, halve, and core the pears (a melon baller works well for this last step). Without cutting through the top ½ inch of the pear, slice each half lengthwise four or five times.

In a large ovenproof skillet, preferably cast iron, heat the butter over medium heat until melted. Stir in the sugar. Put one pear half in the center of the pan, domed side down, and arrange the rest of the pear halves in the skillet (also domed sides down) so the slices fan slightly. Let the pears cook, untouched, over medium heat until the sugar has turned a deep, golden caramel color, 15 to 20 minutes. Rotate the skillet if there seem to be any hot spots.

Meanwhile, preheat the oven to 350°F.

MAKE THE CAKE BATTER: Combine the flour, cornmeal, baking powder, and salt in a small bowl.

In a stand mixer or a medium bowl, beat the butter until light and fluffy. Slowly add the sugar and beat again until light and fluffy. Add the eggs one at a time, mixing after each until well incorporated. Add the vanilla and sour cream. Slowly stir in the dry ingredients until just incorporated.

FOR THE PEARS

5 ripe but firm pears

4 tablespoons (½ stick) unsalted butter

½ cup sugar

FOR THE CAKE

1 cup all-purpose flour

½ cup stone-ground cornmeal

1½ teaspoons baking powder

½ teaspoon salt

8 tablespoons (1 stick) unsalted butter, at room temperature

1 cup sugar

2 large eggs, at room temperature

1 teaspoon vanilla extract

½ cup sour cream

*(recipe continues)*

Spread the batter over the pears in the skillet and bake until a tester inserted in the cake comes out clean, about 25 minutes. Let the cake cool for just a few minutes (not too long or the sugar will start to set and the cake will stick to the pan!). Run a knife around the edge of the skillet, top with a large rimmed plate or platter, and, armed with oven mitts, carefully invert the cake onto the plate. Serve warm.

**I request this for Thanksgiving every year.** It's like having the most delicious cloud of pumpkin pie—light and fluffy yet with all the deep flavors of the heavier classic version. Exactly what you want after eating such an indulgent meal. My mom uses a can of One-Pie pumpkin filling—which is completely acceptable—but using your own winter squash puree feels rustic and grown-up.

MAKES 1 (9-INCH) PIE; SERVES 8 TO 10

# Spiced Squash Chiffon Pie

MAKE THE CRUST: Preheat the oven to 375°F.

In a food processor, pulse the flour, butter, and salt until the butter is in pea-sized pieces. Add the ice water and pulse again until just incorporated.

Transfer the dough to a floured surface. Work it into a ball with your hands and then roll it out into a 16-inch round about ⅛ inch thick. Lay the dough over a 9-inch pie pan and remove the excess dough from the edge, leaving about 1 inch to crimp decoratively.

Line the crust with foil and fill with pastry weights or dried beans. Bake until the edges are golden, 15 to 18 minutes. Remove from the oven, remove the foil and weights, and let cool.

MAKE THE FILLING: Combine the gelatin, ½ cup of the sugar, the evaporated milk, and egg yolks in a medium saucepan. Whisk constantly over low heat until the gelatin and sugar dissolve and the mixture thickens slightly, about 5 minutes. Remove the pan from the heat and stir in the squash, salt, nutmeg, ginger, cinnamon, and cloves. Chill the mixture, stirring occasionally, until completely cool.

FOR THE CRUST

1½ cups all-purpose flour, plus more for rolling the dough

12 tablespoons (1½ sticks) unsalted butter, cold, cut into pieces

¼ teaspoon salt

⅓ cup ice water

FOR THE FILLING

1 (¼-ounce) envelope gelatin

¾ cup granulated sugar

⅔ cup evaporated milk

3 large eggs, separated

1½ cups pureed roasted winter squash, such as kabocha or butternut (see opposite), or 1 (15-ounce) can pumpkin puree

1 teaspoon salt

½ teaspoon grated nutmeg

½ teaspoon ground ginger

1 teaspoon ground cinnamon

¼ teaspoon ground cloves

Perfectly Whipped Cream (page 62)

In a stand mixer fitted with the whisk attachment or using a hand mixer, whip the egg whites until stiff but not dry. Gradually add the remaining ¼ cup sugar and then fold in the chilled squash mixture. Pour into the prepared pie shell and chill for at least 4 hours and up to overnight.

Serve topped with big dollops of perfectly whipped cream.

## Roasted Winter Squash

Preheat the oven to 425°F.

Cut the squash in half and remove the seeds. Brush the flesh with ¼ cup olive oil and season each half with 1 teaspoon salt. Put a tablespoon of butter on top of each, wrap individually in foil, and transfer to the oven. Bake until the squash is fork-tender, 25 to 30 minutes. Scoop out the flesh and puree.

# WINTER

—

## FLANNEL, FROST & WOOD SMOKE

*I love winter.* The evening sky is crisper, brighter, and clearer than ever, and when the first gentle snow begins to float through the air, I feel excitement rather than dread for the long cold season that lies ahead.

*I love winter.* Come late February, that's what I have to repeat, like a mantra, beginning to doubt its truthfulness. The frigid temperatures hold their pattern; the ice, snow, and wind have grown cruel and unyielding. It is a season that tests our limits, pushes our buttons, and corrodes our resilience.

How does one survive a winter in Maine? With good food, good friends, a warm fire . . . and plenty of vitamin D and wine! Winter is the ultimate reminder to slow down and calm weary bones. The shortened daylight provokes a reason to hibernate—to go to bed a little earlier and sleep a little later, the labors of summer behind us. The season also lends a good excuse to spend more time at home in our toasty kitchen, preparing hearty dishes and eating them leisurely by candlelight. Whether it's a batch of creamy chowder, slow-cooked meatloaf, or a pot of baked beans that has soaked up sweet molasses and maple after hours in the oven, good food will see us through the season, helping us feel nourished and warm.

## FIRSTS

Warm Olive Oil & Anchovy Dip

Chicken Liver Mousse

Pork & Chicken Liver Terrine

Winter Kale Caesar with Skillet Croutons & Duck Egg

Chowder of Sweet Clams with Shallots & Fingerlings

Fried Oysters with Root Cellar Slaw & Horseradish Mayonnaise

Oysters on the Half Shell

Scallop Crudo with Pickled Shallots & Lemon


## MAINS

Seared Scallops & Grapefruit-Fennel Salad

Cod with Clementine Relish & Rutabaga–Vanilla Bean Puree

Saturday Night Baked Beans with New England Brown Bread

Corned Brisket New England Dinner

Duck Confit with Celery Root Rémoulade

Dad's Meatloaf with Parsnip Puree & Root Cellar Slaw

Tea-Brined Duck Breast with Fried Potato & Warm Lentil Salad

Cast-Iron Chicken with Roasted Lemon & Rosemary

Wood-Fired Winter Sides

> *Roasted Cauliflower with Olives & Red Pepper Flakes*
>
> *Cider-Braised Brussels Sprouts*


## SWEETS

Nanny's Molasses Cookies with Candied Ginger

Bread Pudding with Apricot & Cardamom

Ricotta Fritters with Custard Sauce & Preserves

Frozen Lemon Terrine with Pistachio Brittle

Chocolate Tart with Chocolate Wafer Crust

Gingerbread with Salted Caramel Whipped Cream

**When I discovered bagna cauda**—or warm olive oil and anchovy dip—I was twenty-two and waitressing at the first restaurant I'd worked in since my dad's diner. I was supposed to describe the dish to customers as a "warm bath" (which is what bagna cauda literally means), but I was pretty incredulous that anyone would buy anything described as a warm anchovy bath. Until I tried it. Garlicky, creamy, and salty, this dip is indeed the perfect little bath for all manner of raw vegetables, especially baby turnips, radishes, and carrots.

**MAKES ABOUT 1½ CUPS**

# Warm Olive Oil & Anchovy Dip

3 garlic cloves, well crushed

4 anchovy fillets, in oil

8 tablespoons (1 stick) unsalted butter, at room temperature

½ cup olive oil

Grated zest and juice of ½ lemon

Pepper

Raw vegetables

In a food processor, combine the garlic, anchovies, and butter. With the machine running, slowly add the olive oil, followed by the lemon zest and juice and a few twists of pepper. Transfer the mixture to a small saucepan and heat over low heat until warm; do not boil. Serve the dip warm with raw vegetables.

**I started making this** rich and creamy spread as a way to use up every last bit of the birds that farmers would bring me at the restaurant. Luckily it couldn't be easier—or more delicious on toast.

**MAKES ABOUT 2 CUPS**

# Chicken Liver Mousse

In a large skillet, preferably cast iron, cook the bacon over medium-low heat, turning to brown both sides. When just crisp, remove from the pan, keeping the drippings in the pan, and blot on paper towels.

Heat the bacon drippings over medium-high heat. Season the chicken livers with kosher salt and pepper and add to the hot pan. Brown on each side, about 3 minutes per side; the livers should still be pink in the center. Remove the livers from the pan and blot on paper towels.

Discard the pan drippings and return the skillet to medium heat. Add the olive oil, shallots, Calvados, apple, thyme, allspice, a pinch of kosher salt, and a couple twists of pepper. Cook, stirring frequently, until the shallots and apple are soft, 7 to 10 minutes. Let cool.

Combine the bacon, chicken livers, and apple mixture in a food processor and pulse to blend. Add the butter and, with the processor running, drizzle in the cream until the mixture is smooth and completely incorporated. Add more cream if the mixture seems too thick. You want a spreadable consistency. Season with kosher salt and pepper.

Pass the mixture through a fine-mesh sieve and spoon into ramekins or small bowls. Spread a thin layer of jam on top of each (this will taste delicious but also keeps the mousse from oxidizing, or browning). Cover the ramekins with plastic wrap and chill for at least 6 hours or overnight.

When almost ready to serve, remove the mousse from the fridge and allow it to come to room temperature, about 20 minutes. Sprinkle with Maldon salt and serve.

4 slices thick-cut applewood-smoked bacon

1 pound chicken livers, tough tendons trimmed

Kosher salt and pepper

2 tablespoons olive oil

4 shallots, chopped

¼ cup Calvados or other brandy

1 crisp apple, peeled and diced

2 sprigs of fresh thyme

¼ teaspoon ground allspice

4 tablespoons (½ stick) unsalted butter, at room temperature

¾ cup heavy cream, or more if needed

¼ cup apricot jam

Maldon salt

Terrines fall into the category of dishes that people have been making for hundreds of years—and with good reason. Here, ground meat is infused with flavor from garlic, shallots, thyme, smoky bacon, and brandy and then layered with chicken livers, prunes, and toasted pistachios before being swaddled in bacon and baked in the oven. Essentially, it's really elegant meatloaf.

While there are entire French texts dedicated to making a "proper" terrine, this is how I like to do it. I also prefer to let a terrine sit overnight in the fridge to let the flavors come together, and serve it just chilled (*not* screaming cold from the fridge) or even at room temperature. Then I give it good company with toast, Maldon salt, cornichons, and sharp mustard. Or I'll turn the whole affair into a decadent charcuterie board with Chicken Liver Mousse (page 195), Warm Olive Oil & Anchovy Dip (page 194), and Radishes & Butter (page 24).

**SERVES 8 TO 12**

# Pork & Chicken Liver Terrine

Finely chop 4 of the bacon strips. In a large bowl, combine the chopped bacon, fatback, ground pork, garlic, shallot, eggs, cream, Calvados, thyme, and parsley. Mix with your hands until well incorporated and almost sticky-feeling, but do not overmix. Season with the salt and pepper and mix to incorporate. Cover with plastic and refrigerate overnight.

Preheat the oven to 325°F.

Line a 9 × 5-inch loaf pan or terrine dish (which come in a variety of sizes and are longer and more slender—and more elegant—than a loaf pan) with the remaining 12 strips of bacon, arranging them crosswise and leaving a 1-inch overhang on the long sides of the dish.

Spread half of the pork mixture in the dish. Arrange the chicken livers in a line on top, followed by the prunes. Sprinkle with the pistachios. Cover

16 thin strips of bacon

½ pound fatback, cut into small pieces

2 pounds ground pork

2 garlic cloves, crushed

1 shallot, diced

2 large eggs

2 tablespoons heavy cream

2 teaspoons Calvados or other good apple brandy

1 tablespoon fresh thyme leaves

2 tablespoons chopped fresh parsley

1 teaspoon salt

6 to 8 twists of pepper

4 chicken livers

8 pitted prunes

¼ cup pistachios, toasted

*(recipe continues)*

with the remaining pork mixture and fold the bacon overhangs over the top.

Wrap the terrine tightly in foil and put the dish inside a larger, high-sided baking dish. Pour boiling water around the terrine to come halfway up the sides, creating a water bath. Bake until an instant-read thermometer inserted into the center registers 155°F, about 1½ hours.

Remove the terrine from the water bath, put it on a rimmed baking sheet, and set a brick on top to help compact the terrine so it will slice nicely. Let cool to room temperature.

Unwrap the terrine, drain off any excess juices, and unmold it. Wrap the terrine in plastic and refrigerate overnight so the flavors can intensify and the terrine can firm up.

To serve, slice the terrine into 1-inch slabs.

**Kale in the winter is the most magical thing** because of its ability to handle frost. It's not only resilient, but all the cold condenses its sugars, leaving the leaves tender and sweet. I think it's the one time of the year when you can pleasantly eat it raw. I like to toss it with a Caesar-inspired anchovy dressing, free-form croutons, long shavings of pecorino, and a warm poached duck egg, which has a bigger, thicker, creamier yolk than a chicken's. That's a perfect winter salad right there.

SERVES 4

# Winter Kale Caesar
## WITH SKILLET CROUTONS & DUCK EGG

2 white anchovy fillets, plus more for serving

1 garlic clove, crushed

Salt and pepper

1 duck egg yolk, or a large chicken yolk

½ teaspoon Dijon mustard

¼ cup olive oil

⅓ cup vegetable oil

Juice of ½ lemon

⅓ cup pecorino shavings

1½ cups torn bread, preferably a good, crusty sourdough

4 good handfuls of baby kale

Lemon wedges

In a medium bowl, combine the anchovies, garlic, and ½ teaspoon salt. Use a fork to mash the ingredients into a paste or pulse until combined. Whisk in the egg yolk and mustard (or pulse again). Drop by drop, whisk in 2 tablespoons of the olive oil to emulsify or drizzle it in as the food processor is running. Then slowly whisk or drizzle in the vegetable oil. Last, mix in the lemon juice and 2 tablespoons of the pecorino. Taste for seasoning and adjust the salt and pepper as needed.

In a small skillet, preferably cast iron, heat the remaining 2 tablespoons olive oil over medium heat. Add the torn bread and cook, stirring frequently, until golden brown.

Transfer the croutons to a large salad bowl. Add the kale and toss with the dressing to coat. Sprinkle with the remaining pecorino shavings and serve with extra anchovies and lemon wedges on the side.

# Chowder of Sweet Clams
## WITH SHALLOTS & FINGERLINGS

**Where I live in Maine,** many people heat their home with a wood-fired stove. It is a lovely throwback to the way things used to be, is less expensive than oil, and makes for the ultimate gathering place. That said, *stacking* wood is no joke. Assuming you've already taken the shortcut of ordering your firewood (rather than cutting down the trees yourself, splitting the wood, and letting it dry all summer—a yearlong process that's not uncommon practice around here), you still need to arrange the logs in your woodshed in a way that allows them to dry out further and burn more efficiently. This in theory might not sound like much of an undertaking, but if you consider that a cord of wood is 4 feet high and 8 feet long, and that it takes roughly 5 or 6 cords to heat a modestly sized house, then suddenly stacking wood doesn't seem so quaint. It's a ritual meant for Saturday or Sunday afternoons, calling together all your friends and family (if you're smart), and taking the better part of the day to brace for the storms to come.

And after that, it's time to put the chowder on. You can get the prep done and shallots caramelizing during stacking breaks, then treat everyone to a warm bowl and a beer. Serve with From-Scratch Saltines (page 34).

**SERVES 4 TO 6**

5 pounds clams, either steamers or littlenecks

1 pound baby potatoes

Salt and pepper

3 tablespoons olive oil, plus more for serving

6 shallots, thinly sliced

3 cups heavy cream

2 cups whole milk

6 tablespoons (¾ stick) unsalted butter

Juice of 1 lemon

2 tablespoons chopped fresh parsley

2 tablespoons chopped fresh dill

Give the clams a good rinse under cold running water, discarding any with cracked shells, and put them in a large pot with a lid. Add 2½ cups water to the pot, cover, and cook over high heat until the clams steam open, about 5 minutes. Drain and let cool to room temperature. Use an oyster or clam knife to shuck the clams, discarding any that didn't open. Reserve the clam meat.

Wipe out the pot and add the potatoes. Pour in just enough cold water to cover and season with salt. Bring the water to a boil, then reduce the heat so the water simmers, and cook the potatoes until fork-tender, 10 to 12 minutes. Drain the potatoes and let cool to room temperature before cutting into bite-sized pieces.

Return the pot to medium heat and add the olive oil and shallots. Cook, stirring frequently, until deeply caramelized, about 20 minutes. Add the potatoes, cream, milk, and butter and bring to a gentle simmer. Add the clams and lemon juice and season with salt and pepper to taste. Cook for another minute, just to heat the clams through.

Remove the pot from the heat, sprinkle in the parsley and dill, drizzle with a bit of olive oil, and serve.

**This is a cold-weather version** of your classic fried oyster basket, served up in one neat little bite.

**SERVES 4**

# Fried Oysters
## WITH ROOT CELLAR SLAW & HORSERADISH MAYONNAISE

Vegetable oil, for frying

12 oysters

1 cup semolina flour

1 cup all-purpose flour

Maldon salt

Pepper

Root Cellar Slaw (page 226)

Horseradish Mayo (page 37)

Fennel fronds, for garnish (optional)

Heat oil in a deep fryer to 375°F or, alternatively, heat 2 inches of oil in a heavy-bottomed pan to the same temperature.

As the oil heats, shuck the oysters (see page 204). Instead of leaving the oyster meat on the shells, though, put it and the liquor in a bowl. Rinse the cupped bottom shells with water and reserve.

In a medium bowl, combine the semolina and all-purpose flours. Remove the oyster meat from the liquor and lightly dredge in the semolina mixture. Working in 2 batches, drop the oysters into the oil and fry for 30 seconds or until just golden. Drain on paper towels and sprinkle with Maldon salt and pepper.

Set the cleaned oyster shells on a surface where they won't wobble. A mounded tablespoon of coarse salt works well, or you can get creative and use things like small stones or seaweed. Scoop a generous tuft of slaw on each shell, top with an oyster and a dollop of mayo, and garnish with a whisp of fennel frond, if desired. Serve immediately.

# Oysters on the Half Shell

Let's face it: oysters are intimidating. Their foreign, muddy, oddly misshapen shells—no two exactly alike—can be hard to make heads or tails of. But don't let these mollusks fool you! With a few quick tips and a little patience, they are, in fact, quite simple to master and enjoy at home.

Remember that oysters are living creatures. Do not suffocate them by storing them in an airtight container. Keep them refrigerated in a bowl covered with a clean cloth until you're ready to shuck. Well-kept oysters can last over a week in the fridge.

You will need:

- Rough brush or towel for cleaning

- Oyster knife

- Clean towel

- Metal mesh glove (optional)

- Chilled platter filled with crushed ice

- 3 or 4 fresh oysters in the shell per person (I always figure most people will eat about that many, one person won't have any, and then some guy or gal will throw back a dozen. The lovers and the haters balance each other out.)

Clean the oysters. Scrub them under cold running water using a rough brush or towel to remove mud and debris from their shells. Take notice of the oyster's shape and you will see that one side is rounded while the other is relatively flatter. The rounded side is the bottom of the oyster and the flat end is the top—the part of the shell that you'll be removing. Also observe the "point" of the oyster, or the place where the two shells meet to form a point. This is also called the hinge or the "key" and is, not surprisingly, the key to getting into the oyster.

Before you pick up an oyster knife, remember that even though it doesn't look like other knives in your kitchen, it's still sharp. Take your time and use good sense just as you would with any other kitchen task that has the potential of injury. A mesh glove will lend extra protection for slips, but it's by no means necessary. A kitchen towel will also offer some protection.

Put the oyster rounded-side down on a clean folded towel with the key of the oyster pointing toward your dominant hand. Wrap the towel up over the non-key side of the oyster and keep your other hand securely across the towel and oyster. Put the tip of your oyster knife directly at the oyster's key. Gently begin working the oyster knife into the key, angling the blade down into the cup of the oyster, rocking it back and forth a bit, discarding any debris as it comes loose. This isn't a function of brute force so much as it is angles. When you feel the key give and the knife sink in, twist it as if you were turning a key in an ignition until you feel the hinge pop.

Loosen the remainder of the shell by running the knife around the top shell, keeping your knife parallel to the table so that it also detaches the oyster meat from the top of the shell. Remove the top shell and run your knife gently under the oyster meat to detach it from the bottom shell, leaving the oyster in place. Bring the shell and oyster to your nose and take a sniff. It should smell salty and clean and be plump and surrounded by liquid. Anything else should be thrown away. (When in doubt, throw it out.) Put the shucked oyster on the platter of crushed ice, being mindful not to lose any of the delicious juices or "liquor." Enjoy immediately, either on its own, with a squeeze of lemon, or topped with mignonette sauce or flavored ices (recipes on page 208). Or set up a Working Man's raw bar (see page 209).

# MIGNONETTE SAUCE

Mignonette sauce is nothing but vinegar, shallot, and black pepper, and it's a staple on my table. Unlike cocktail sauce, which completely smothers an oyster, mignonette brings out its brightness and clean, briny flavor. Otherwise, you might as well be having a shot of horseradish and ketchup! Mignonette is also the perfect canvas for all kinds of other flavors that complement oysters. You can add herbs, such as chives and thyme, a hint of horseradish and tomato for a Bloody Mary take (or for what I like to call "cocktail sauce recovery"), or, like in the variation at right, some hibiscus flowers to give it a beautiful deep red color. While there's no rule about what kind of vinegar to use in a mignonette, I prefer seasoned rice wine vinegar, which has a little salt and sugar added to it.

Put the shallot in a small jar, cover with the vinegar, and add the pepper. Secure the lid and refrigerate until chilled. The sauce will keep for up to 1 week in the refrigerator.

MAKES ABOUT ½ CUP

1 medium shallot, finely diced

½ cup seasoned rice wine vinegar

½ teaspoon pepper

**Hibiscus Mignonette**

Heat the vinegar in a small saucepan over medium-high heat. Remove from the heat just as bubbles begin to form. Add 2 teaspoons dried hibiscus flowers and steep for 1 minute. Strain the mixture through a fine-mesh sieve and discard the hibiscus flowers. Let the infused vinegar cool to room temperature, then mix with the shallots and pepper. Refrigerate to chill, about 30 minutes.

# BEETROOT-HORSERADISH FLAVORED ICE

There's nothing better than an icy cold oyster, except perhaps one subtly flavored—and colored—with an earthy, spice-infused ice.

Combine the beet juice, horseradish, lemon juice, and salt in a small ramekin and freeze until solid. Scrape with a fork to break it up into a granita-like consistency. Return to the freezer until ready to serve.

MAKES ABOUT ½ CUP

½ cup beet juice, homemade or store-bought

1 teaspoon prepared horseradish

Juice of ½ lemon

Pinch of salt

## Raw Bar Anytime, All the Time

A big misconception about a spread of raw oysters and other seafood is that it's something that should be reserved for fancy occasions. But I hereby give you permission to have friends over on a weeknight in November to do this. No champagne fountain required—just bottles of beer or jelly jars of Prosecco.

Another common fallacy is that a raw bar is a summer thing. But most items that you'd find on those tiered platters are at their peak season during cold weather—or in months that have an "r" in their names (September through April).

Since there's not much to a platter of oysters, I like to make the presentation special. Look for a good-sized vintage platter, galvanized tray, or wide shallow bowl—I love the washbasins that used to be paired with a pitcher on a nightstand for washing up—or even a slab of driftwood or clean barn board. Put down a bed of salt, seaweed, crushed ice, or (my favorite) snow, and arrange the oysters on top. Garnish with whatever is natural and free: stones, shells, or cedar, juniper, or evergreen branches.

Other nice additions to a raw bar:

- Stone crab claws: Buy these already cooked from your fishmonger and serve them with a flavored mayonnaise (see page 37). Tarragon would be delicious.

- Clams on the half shell: You'll need a clam knife, which is pointier and sharper than an oyster knife, but shucking is almost exactly the same (see page 204), albeit a bit harder. This is a job best left for your fishmonger if you are uninitiated.

- Lobster: Cook up some 11-Minute Lobster (page 102), halve the tails lengthwise, and crack the claws. Serve with melted butter and lemon.

The first time I saw my dad eating scallops raw at the diner, I thought it was the craziest thing. He'd get them by the gallon, pull off the white plastic lid, and just throw them back by the dozen. Of course, by the time I was an adult I understood that it was no different from eating sushi, and once I tasted a fresh-from-the-ocean, still-squirming scallop, I understood how a gallon of them could not possibly be enough. They're delicate, plump, sweet, salty, and clean. It's no wonder that people often request double orders whenever I have raw scallops on the menu.

Essentially, crudo is the Italian version of sashimi—or beautiful, perfect, raw scallops sliced thin and served simply like they are here: with shallot, a little jalapeño for heat, lemon juice and zest, and really good olive oil. Needless to say, it's crucial that you use the freshest scallops possible (see page 212).

SERVES 6 (OR MAYBE 1)

# Scallop Crudo
## WITH PICKLED SHALLOTS & LEMON

2 teaspoons finely diced shallot

1 teaspoon finely chopped fresh ginger

1 teaspoon finely chopped seeded jalapeño

1 tablespoon seasoned rice wine vinegar

½ pound super-fresh day-boat sea scallops

Grated zest and juice of ½ lemon

Olive oil

¼ cup microgreens, for garnish (optional)

Combine the shallot, ginger, and jalapeño in a small bowl. Add the rice wine vinegar and allow to macerate for 15 minutes.

Slice the scallops horizontally into about 4 rounds per scallop. Arrange on a chilled platter and spoon the shallot mixture over the top. Sprinkle with the lemon zest and juice and drizzle with olive oil. Garnish with microgreens, if using, and serve immediately.

**Whereas raw scallops are sexy, soft, and delicate,** their seared counterparts are meaty, juicy, and rich. Cooked for mere seconds in a cast-iron pan and basted with butter (which melds with the scallops' natural brine to make the easiest-ever pan sauce), seared scallops are the best party trick because you don't have to stand at the stove for long to put out a dish that's refined, bright, and totally delicious. Serve as-is for a casual dinner or make smaller portions for an elegant starter or first course for eight to ten people.

**SERVES 6**

# Seared Scallops
## & GRAPEFRUIT-FENNEL SALAD

1 fennel bulb, shaved

2 grapefruits, segmented (see page 215), juice reserved

2 tablespoons Macerated Shallot Vinaigrette (page 30)

Handful of purple mustard greens or arugula

Olive oil

Salt

1½ pounds day-boat sea scallops

4 tablespoons (½ stick) unsalted butter

Make the salad by tossing the fennel and grapefruit segments with the macerated shallot vinaigrette in a medium bowl. Mound the mixture in the middle of a platter. Use the same bowl to dress the greens with a drizzle of olive oil and a sprinkle of salt. Use your hands—the greens should feel lightly coated. Scatter the greens on the platter around the fennel.

Lay the scallops on a paper towel to gently blot any excess moisture. Lightly salt the tops. Heat 2 large skillets, preferably cast iron, over medium-high heat and pour 2 tablespoons olive oil into each. Arrange the scallops in the pans, salted-side down, so they're not touching. Sear the scallops until golden brown, about a minute and a half. Sprinkle the scallops with salt, then flip and cook for another 30 seconds.

Add 2 tablespoons butter to each skillet and cook for another minute, until the scallops are barely cooked through. Remove the pans from the heat and arrange the scallops on top of the salad. Drizzle with some of the pan juices and a bit of the reserved grapefruit juice.

**A Quick Guide to Scallops**

You want to find sushi-grade scallops, especially if you're serving them raw. And always ask when they've been caught—ideally that day, or the day before at most. If they smell like the ocean and are glossy and bubbling, then they're what you're looking for.

To prep them for cooking, all you have to do is remove what I call the belly button but is technically known as the "foot" or abductor muscle. It's a small white tag that's a little more opaque than the scallop's flesh and harder in texture. Just pull it off with your fingers.

**I love cooking cod.** It's thick and flaky and couldn't be easier to prepare. In fact, once you master this simple technique, you can cook the perfect piece of fish—no matter what kind—every single time. If you can't find cod, you could easily substitute hake or halibut. Though this flavor combination might sound a little odd, it's actually one of my favorites: the cod is buttery and the puree (perfumed with a hint of vanilla) is earthy and rich, while the bright citrus relish holds everything in balance.

**SERVES 6**

# Cod with Clementine Relish
## & RUTABAGA-VANILLA BEAN PUREE

1 skin-on cod fillet (about 4 pounds)

Salt

Olive oil, plus more for serving

4 tablespoons (½ stick) unsalted butter

Rutabaga–Vanilla Bean Puree (opposite)

Clementine Relish (opposite)

Preheat the oven to 425°F.

Slice the cod fillet into 6 portions. Pat the skin dry with a paper towel and season each fillet with salt.

You don't want to overcrowd your skillets when cooking fish (it'll steam instead of getting golden and crispy), so I recommend cooking in batches. Heat 2 large ovenproof skillets, preferably cast iron, over high heat and put a tablespoon of olive oil in each. Once the oil just begins to smoke, add the fish, skin-side down. Sear until the skin is golden brown, 3 to 4 minutes.

Flip the fish over and add 2 tablespoons butter to each skillet. Transfer the pans to the oven. Cook the fish until flaky and just barely opaque in the middle, 8 to 10 minutes.

To serve, scoop rutabaga puree onto each plate, top with a piece of fish, and spoon the clementine relish and juice over the fish. I also like to drizzle a bit of good olive oil around the border of the plate.

# RUTABAGA–VANILLA BEAN PUREE

Rutabaga can be an overpowering root vegetable, but the vanilla tempers that edge and gives it an almost feminine softness. You can make this puree ahead and reheat it in a double boiler.

Put the rutabaga in a medium saucepan with just enough cold water to cover, season with salt, and bring to a boil over high heat. Reduce the heat so that the water simmers and cook the rutabaga until fork-tender, 10 to 12 minutes.

Drain the rutabaga and transfer it to a food processor. Add the butter and vanilla bean seeds. While the food processor is running, slowly pour in the cream and continue processing until smooth. Season with salt and pepper to taste.

SERVES 6 WITH
LEFTOVERS

1 rutabaga or 2 or
3 white turnips
(1½ to 2 pounds),
roughly chopped

Salt and pepper

4 tablespoons (½ stick)
unsalted butter

1 vanilla bean, split
lengthwise and scraped

½ cup heavy cream

# CLEMENTINE RELISH

When you're getting into the winter months and it's a constant struggle to find bright, fresh flavors, citrus is one answer. It might not be citrus season in Maine, but it is elsewhere. I gladly welcome some vibrant color and brightness any day this time of year.

Slice off the top and bottom of each clementine and squeeze the ends' juice into a small bowl.

Set each clementine cut-side down on your cutting board. Run a paring knife from top to bottom, removing just the outer peel and pith (discard). Slice between each clementine's membranes to extract single segments of fruit. Put the segments in the small bowl with the juice and squeeze out any remaining juice from the membrane that's left over.

Add the thyme and vinaigrette and stir gently to blend. I like to serve this the day I make it so that the citrus does not start to lose its flavor.

MAKES 1 CUP

4 clementines

1 teaspoon fresh thyme
leaves

1 tablespoon Macerated
Shallot Vinaigrette
(page 30)

Every Saturday, my mother's bean crock—filled with dried beans, salt pork, a little maple syrup—would go on the stove and a tin of B&M brown bread would go in the oven. It's a combination that screams New England and is a cherished food memory—one this book simply wouldn't be complete without. Serve with Waldorf Salad with Apples, Fennel & Candied Walnuts (page 157) for a true Freedom experience.

**SERVES 8**

# Saturday Night Baked Beans
## WITH NEW ENGLAND BROWN BREAD

Preheat the oven to 250°F.

Fill a medium pot with just enough water to cover the beans. Add 2 tablespoons salt, bring to a boil, and reduce the heat so that the water simmers. Cook the beans for 25 minutes, just long enough to soften them.

As the beans simmer, heat a large skillet, preferably cast iron, over medium heat. Fry the salt pork, turning to brown all sides, 5 to 6 minutes total.

Transfer the pork to a plate, leaving the rendered fat in the pan. Add the onion to the pan with a pinch of salt and cook to soften, about 5 minutes.

1½ pounds dried beans, soaked overnight and drained (see Note)

Salt and pepper

½ pound salt pork

1 medium onion, diced

½ cup ketchup

½ cup molasses

½ cup maple syrup, plus more for drizzling

2 tablespoons apple cider vinegar

1 tablespoon dry mustard

1½ cups packed light brown sugar

About 4 cups boiling water

New England Brown Bread (opposite)

**Note**

Marfax beans are classic and the creamiest here, but you could also use navy beans or another dried bean of choice. If you buy a 2-pound bag, save the leftovers for blind baking piecrusts.

Put the salt pork and onion in a large bowl. Drain the beans and add them to the bowl. Stir in the ketchup, molasses, maple syrup, vinegar, mustard, brown sugar, 1 teaspoon salt, and a few twists of pepper. Transfer the mixture to a bean pot or large Dutch oven. Pour in just enough boiling water to cover the beans, stir to combine, and bake for 5 to 6 hours, until the beans are tender but not falling apart. Check occasionally to see if you need to add more boiling water so the beans don't dry out.

Season to taste and serve with brown bread and a drizzle of maple syrup, if desired.

# NEW ENGLAND BROWN BREAD

This simple, no-knead bread couldn't be easier to make. I bake mine the old-fashioned way, in a 39-ounce coffee can, but you could also use a regular loaf pan.

Preheat the oven to 350°F. Grease a 9 x 5-inch loaf pan with butter.

Combine the all-purpose flour, rye flour, cornmeal, baking soda, baking powder, salt, and sugar in a large bowl. Stir in the milk, molasses, and vanilla and fold in the raisins.

Pour the dough into the loaf pan and cover with foil. Set the loaf pan inside a larger baking dish and fill about halfway with boiling water. This will help keep the bread moist as it bakes. Bake until a tester inserted in the center comes out clean, 25 to 30 minutes.

Let the bread cool slightly in the pan, then run a knife around the edge and gently remove the bread. Cool at least slightly on a wire rack before serving with plenty of soft butter.

MAKES 1 (9 X 5-INCH) LOAF

Unsalted butter, at room temperature, for greasing the pan and slathering the bread

½ cup all-purpose flour

½ cup rye flour

½ cup cornmeal

1 teaspoon baking soda

1 teaspoon baking powder

1 teaspoon salt

1 tablespoon sugar

1 cup whole milk

⅓ cup dark molasses

1 teaspoon vanilla extract

½ cup golden raisins

2 cups boiling water

If I had to pick one last meal on my deathbed, it would be either lobster or corned beef—and I'd probably go with the latter. What can I say? I'm a sucker for cured and slow-cooked cuts of cheap meat. My grandparents always made me a traditional New England boiled dinner on my birthday, simmering the corned beef for hours with carrots, potatoes, turnips, and pickling spices like coriander and black pepper. Then everything was spooned onto a platter and served up family-style. That's my kind of winter dish.

Note that this dish calls for two days of curing.

**SERVES 6**

# Corned Brisket
# New England Dinner

Make a brine by combining 1 gallon water with the salt, sugar, ¼ cup of the pickling spices, and the garlic in a large pot. Bring it to a boil, then remove from heat and let cool completely.

Add the brisket to the brine, using a plate to keep it submerged. Refrigerate for 2 days to cure.

Remove the brisket from the brine and rinse. Put the brisket in a clean stockpot, cover with water, and add the remaining ¼ cup pickling spices. Bring to a boil, then reduce to a gentle simmer. Cover and cook until tender, about 4 hours.

Toss in the potatoes, carrots, turnips, and cabbage and continue to simmer until the vegetables are just tender, 10 to 15 minutes.

Strain the meat and vegetables from the cooking liquid. Slice the meat across the grain and arrange it on a platter alongside the veggies. Sprinkle with the parsley and cilantro and serve with butter, Maldon salt, pepper, mustard, and apple cider vinegar as condiments.

1 cup kosher salt

¾ cup packed light brown sugar

½ cup pickling spices

6 garlic cloves, smashed

1 beef brisket (about 5 pounds)

1 pound potatoes, peeled (small potatoes are fantastic, but big white ones will do, too; just quarter them)

1 pound carrots, peeled

1 pound turnips, peeled and diced

1 small head of green cabbage (about 1 pound), cut into 4 wedges

1 tablespoon chopped fresh parsley

1 tablespoon chopped fresh cilantro

Unsalted butter

Maldon salt and pepper

Dijon mustard

Apple cider vinegar

**Slow-cooking duck in its own fat** and pairing it with a bright, crisp salad is just one way of bringing slow-cooked love to a plate as well as adding some freshness of the season. In this case it's a celery root rémoulade, whose creamy brininess perfectly balances the richness of the duck. This dish is light enough to serve for a celebratory lunch, yet still substantial enough for supper.

Even though I call for deep-frying the duck confit here—yes, please!—you can skip that step altogether and still have a sumptuous dish. Just make sure to pull the meat from the bone and discard the skin; otherwise the texture's not as lovely.

SERVES 6

# Duck Confit
## WITH CELERY ROOT RÉMOULADE

4 garlic cloves, sliced

1 large shallot, sliced

¼ cup herbes de Provence

¼ cup kosher salt

6 duck legs (about 5 pounds total)

4 cups rendered duck fat, melted

Vegetable oil, for frying

In a large bowl, combine the garlic, shallot, herbs, and salt; rub the mixture over the duck legs. Cover and cure in the refrigerator for 24 hours.

Preheat the oven to 250°F.

Gently brush the salt mixture from the duck legs and put them in an ovenproof ceramic or glass baking dish big enough to accommodate the legs in a single layer. Pour in the duck fat so the legs are submerged. Transfer to the oven and cook until the duck is light golden and cooked through, about 4 hours. Allow the duck to cool to room temperature while still submerged in the fat.

If serving this dish the same day you've prepared the confit, then remove the duck from the fat, transfer it to a cooling rack set on top of a baking sheet, and refrigerate for an hour to dry out slightly. (This extra step is required only for just-confited duck.)

However, if serving this dish the next day (or another day; this duck will last for a while in the fridge if left submerged in fat), simply refrigerate it.

When ready to serve, heat vegetable oil in a deep fryer to 375°F or, alternatively, heat 2 inches of oil in a heavy-bottomed pan to the same temperature.

Remove the duck legs from the fat and, working in batches, fry until golden brown and warmed through, 3 to 4 minutes. Put them on paper towels to absorb some of the excess oil.

Serve over a bed of rémoulade. Devour with your hands, or a knife and fork if you insist.

## CELERY ROOT RÉMOULADE

Rémoulade—or creamy slaw—calls for celery root tossed in a mayonnaise-based dressing brightened with Dijon mustard and capers. It's a surprising hint of sunshine for a vegetable that looks as though it's seen none.

In a large bowl, whisk together the mayo, cream, and mustard.

Peel the celery root and grate it on the finest setting of a mandoline or cut it into thin matchsticks by hand with a sharp knife. Add the celery root to the bowl with the dressing along with the cornichons and parsley. Stir to coat. Add a bit more cream if the mixture seems dry. Season with salt and pepper to taste.

SERVES 6

⅓ cup mayonnaise, homemade (page 37) or store-bought

2 tablespoons heavy cream, or more if needed

1 tablespoon Dijon mustard

1 medium celery root

¼ cup chopped cornichons

2 tablespoons chopped fresh parsley

Salt and pepper

When I was away at college, this is the dish I craved the most. It is my dad's recipe, one that he taught me how to make in the diner. I put my own spin on it and frequently treat myself to this on chilly nights with a baked potato and sour cream—or, for this more refined version, a bed of magenta slaw or a silky parsnip puree.

SERVES 8

# Dad's Meatloaf
WITH PARSNIP PUREE & ROOT CELLAR SLAW

Preheat the oven to 375°F.

START THE MEATLOAF: Combine all of the meatloaf ingredients in a large bowl and use your hands to mix them until just evenly combined. Do not overmix. Divide the mixture between two 9 × 5-inch loaf pans.

MAKE THE GLAZE: In a medium bowl, stir together all of the ingredients.

Brush the top of each meatloaf with a thick coat of the glaze. Transfer to the oven and bake until an instant-read thermometer reads 150°F, 45 minutes.

Let the meatloaf rest for 10 to 15 minutes, then unmold, cut into slices, and serve with the slaw and parsnip puree, if desired.

## FOR THE MEATLOAF

1½ pounds ground beef

1½ pounds ground pork

¾ cup shredded carrot

½ cup chopped shallots

½ cup shredded pecorino

2 cups ½-inch bread cubes, such as crusty sourdough

2 tablespoons fresh thyme leaves

2 large eggs

½ cup whole milk

2 teaspoons salt

6 to 8 twists of pepper

## FOR THE GLAZE

½ cup packed light brown sugar

¾ cup ketchup

1 tablespoon Dijon mustard

Root Cellar Slaw (page 226, optional)

Parsnip Puree (page 226, optional)

## ROOT CELLAR SLAW

I make this dish when I'm dreaming of summer days on a winter night. It lets storage vegetables give any dish that raw, fresh crunch that's such a luxury in the cold season. You can use just about any root vegetables—beets, parsnips, celery root, turnips—but I look to purple cabbage, purple carrots, and Chioggia beets to lend their deep, earthy color and flavor. Finish it off with a sprinkle of thyme, dill, marjoram, or whatever fresh herbs you can get your hands on.

Grate the beets and carrots on the fine matchstick setting of a mandoline. You could use a box grater, but it won't have as sexy a finish. Finely slice the cabbage.

Combine the vegetables in a large bowl and toss with the shallot vinaigrette and olive oil. Let the mixture sit for at least 15 minutes so the flavors can infuse. Fold in the herbs and season with salt and pepper.

SERVES 8

1 medium red beet, peeled

1 medium Chioggia beet, peeled

4 large purple carrots, peeled

1 small head purple cabbage (about 1½ pounds)

Macerated Shallot Vinaigrette (page 30)

2 tablespoons olive oil

2 tablespoons chopped fresh herbs

Salt and pepper

## PARSNIP PUREE

This is a lot like mashed potatoes—but better. Parsnips have a hint of nuttiness that's not found in your standard mashed starch. And they're more luxurious because you can puree them into a creamy silk, which you can't do with potatoes or they'll get gummy. But most beautiful—all you have to do is boil the parsnips in salted water until tender, then pop them into a food processor or blender with cream, butter, and salt. That's it. Pair this puree with chicken, duck, beef, or fish.

Put the parsnips in a medium saucepan, add cold water to cover, and season with salt. Bring to a boil, then reduce the heat so that the water simmers, and cook until just fork-tender, about 20 minutes.

Drain the parsnips and transfer to a food processor. Add the butter and pulse until melted. Pour in the cream and process until very smooth. Taste and add salt if needed, though if your cooking water is well seasoned, you likely won't need more. Serve right away or keep warm in a double boiler.

SERVES 8

3 pounds parsnips, peeled and roughly chopped

Salt

4 tablespoons (½ stick) unsalted butter

½ cup heavy cream, warmed

## Love Craft

# HANDMADE NAPKINS

I recently found a sweater in the attic of my parents' house. It was more than fifty years old, knit by my grandmother for my aunt. Preserved in perfect condition, it was a precious memory of my grandmother and her soft yet hardworking hands. Over the decades it has been enjoyed by countless family members; I wore it as a little girl, and it once perfectly fit my ten-year-old son. He wore it proudly (on special occasions only), knowing that he was being kept cozy by the craft of his great-grandmother, whom he was lucky enough to know, albeit briefly.

I like to think of my cooking as a similar sort of craft. With it, I found the power to comfort and to provide warmth and love. Even though a dish is only temporary, I can embrace the memories of a great meal and the company with whom I shared it. Recipes from my past also connect me to my childhood.

Whatever your craft might be, put it out there for all to enjoy. If you are looking to try your hand at a new craft, make some napkins. Here's my mother's "recipe" for simple, everyday ones.

**MAKES 4 NAPKINS**

**YOU WILL NEED:**

Iron and ironing board

Gridded fabric cutting mat

Marking pen

Scissors

Rotary cutter (optional)

1 yard of fabric, preshrunk

24-inch sewing ruler

Pins

Coordinating thread

Preheat the iron on its highest setting.

Using the gridded fabric-cutting mat, marking pen, and scissors (or rotary cutter), cut four 18-inch squares from the fabric.

Press all 4 corners 1½ inches toward the underside of the fabric, then trim ½ inch off each corner.

Fold each edge of the fabric ½ inch toward the underside of the material and press flat with the iron. Fold again another ½ inch so that corners meet. Press flat and pin in place.

At this stage you may proceed with a sewing machine or go about it the old-fashioned way, sewing by hand. Stitch around the inside hem, leaving a $\frac{1}{16}$-inch seam allowance. Repeat this step, stitching ⅛ inch around the outer edge. Then repeat on the remaining three squares of fabric.

Smoky Lapsang souchong is just amazing when added to a brine. It's a natural way to add some kissed-by-fire flavor to meat when you don't have a fancy smoker. This duck manages to taste like it has spent all day cooking low and slow. It's the perfect trick for making an impressive dinner for friends with very little effort.

SERVES 6

# Tea-Brined Duck Breast
## WITH FRIED POTATO & WARM LENTIL SALAD

⅓ cup kosher salt

⅓ cup sugar

⅓ cup Lapsang souchong tea leaves

4 duck breasts (10 to 12 ounces each)

Fried Potato & Warm Lentil Salad (page 231, optional)

Make a brine by combining the salt and sugar with 1 quart water in a large pot. Bring to a boil, add the tea, and remove the pot from the heat. Let the mixture steep for 15 to 20 minutes. Strain the tea by pouring it through a fine-mesh sieve into a bowl or pot large enough to hold the duck; discard the tea leaves. Cool the reserved liquid completely.

Score the duck skin, which will help the duck soak up the flavorful brine as well as help the fat render and make the skin nice and crispy. Gently draw your knife across the breast on a diagonal at ¼-inch intervals, taking care to slice only through the skin and not the meat. Rotate the breast 90 degrees and repeat, making a diamond pattern.

Submerge the duck in the brine and refrigerate for 8 hours or overnight.

Remove the duck from the brine, put it on a rimmed baking sheet, and refrigerate for an hour to let it dry out. This will help the skin get crispy.

Preheat the oven to 425°F.

Heat 2 large ovenproof skillets, preferably cast iron, over medium-high heat. Divide the duck breasts between the 2 pans, laying them skin-side down. Keep a small bowl nearby so that as the fat renders, you can collect it periodically and discard. Cook, without turning, until the skin is golden brown, 4 to 6 minutes.

*(recipe continues)*

Drain any remaining excess fat from the pans and transfer to the oven. Cook until the duck is medium rare or an instant-read thermometer reads 135°F, 5 to 8 minutes, depending on the size of your duck breasts. Remove the breasts from the oven and allow to rest for 5 to 10 minutes.

Slice each breast crosswise; you should get about 6 slices per breast. Arrange on a platter and serve with the potatoes and lentils.

## Winter Blossoms

Forcing blossoms at home is an easy and inexpensive way to speed up spring and feed the craving for a change of season. Simply take clippings from a spring-blossoming bush or tree such as forsythia, quince, cherry, apple, or magnolia and immerse in a favorite vase filled with warm water. Within a week or two, tiny buds will begin to emerge followed by beautiful blossoms.

Additionally, if you lightly pound the cut ends of the twigs with a hammer before submerging in water, the branches will be able to soak up even more warm water. Replenish the warm water daily to speed things up.

Have faith; spring is on the way. Soon the red-breasted robins will make their seasonal debut, the days will get longer, and, within a few short weeks, the thaw will begin. Until then, you can force it a bit.

# FRIED POTATO & WARM LENTIL SALAD

I first made this salad when my friend Victoria brought me the most beautiful little fingerling potatoes. I could just see them sliced up into little coins and fried until golden. I also happened to be planning one of the debut dinners at The Mill—a birthday party for our project manager, Jimmy, a notorious meat-and-potato enthusiast. I had to figure out a way to keep this man happy while maybe sneaking in a more interesting element. I decided to go with French lentils, infusing them with garlic and bay leaf before tossing them in a hot skillet with the buttery potatoes. Topped with some ricotta salata for a salty zing and fresh herbs, it made for a happy birthday indeed.

Combine the lentils, bay leaf, shallot, garlic, and 1 tablespoon salt in a medium saucepan. Add cold water to cover by an inch or two and cook over medium heat until the lentils are just tender, about 25 minutes. Take care not to overcook them or they'll turn to mush. Drain the lentils and discard the bay leaf, shallot, and garlic.

Put the potatoes in a medium pot with just enough cold water to cover. Season with salt and bring the water to a boil, then reduce the heat so that the water simmers, and cook the potatoes until fork-tender, 15 to 20 minutes. Drain and set aside to cool. Slice the potatoes into bite-sized coins.

Put the olive oil and butter in a large skillet, preferably cast iron, and heat over medium-high heat. Add the potatoes and season with pepper. Stir to coat and cook, stirring frequently, until the potatoes just start to brown, 2 to 4 minutes.

Add the lentils and shake the pan to keep all of the ingredients moving, cooking until the lentils are just warmed through, about 2 minutes. Add the lemon zest and juice and dill fronds. Give the lot a sprinkle of ricotta, toss once more, and transfer to a serving bowl.

SERVES 6

1 cup du Puy lentils (French green lentils)

1 bay leaf

1 shallot

4 garlic cloves

Salt and pepper

1 pound baby potatoes

2 tablespoons olive oil

2 tablespoons unsalted butter

Grated zest and juice of 1 lemon

¼ cup chopped dill fronds

¼ cup crumbled ricotta salata

There's nothing more satisfying to make for a gathering—or a weeknight supper—than a simple roast chicken. This version takes it to another level. By weighting down the chicken as it roasts, you ensure that it cooks evenly and maintains its succulent juiciness. Add a little butter, lemon, and rosemary to the pan—heaven—and serve with either of the Wood-Fired Winter Sides (pages 234–235). Hey winter, you're not so bad after all.

**SERVES 4**

# Cast-Iron Chicken
## WITH ROASTED LEMON & ROSEMARY

1 whole chicken (3½ to 4 pounds), cut into pieces (see below)

Basic Brine (page 170)

¼ cup olive oil

4 sprigs of fresh rosemary

1 lemon, cut into wedges

6 tablespoons (¾ stick) unsalted butter

Submerge the chicken in the brine, cover, and refrigerate for 24 to 36 hours.

Preheat the oven to 425°F.

Drain the chicken, pat dry with paper towels, and allow it to come to room temperature, about 30 minutes.

Heat the olive oil in a large ovenproof skillet, preferably cast iron, over high heat. Carefully lay the chicken pieces in the pan in a single layer, skin-side down. Cook until you can hear the skin sizzling, about 4 minutes. Put another heavy ovenproof skillet or a foil-wrapped brick on top of the chicken and transfer to the oven. Be strong—it will be heavy! Roast for 8 minutes.

Remove the top skillet and flip the chicken pieces. Add the rosemary, lemon wedges, and butter and continue roasting, uncovered. Cook until the chicken is cooked through and the juices run clear, about 15 minutes.

Let the chicken rest for 5 minutes before serving with the pan juices.

**Cutting a Chicken into Parts**

You want a big, sharp knife for this job. First cut around each leg at the hip joint. Then slice between the leg and thigh. Cut the wing tips off at the joint and discard or save for stock. Cut through the breastbone to halve the chicken lengthwise. Remove the backbone and discard or save for stock. Now you should have two breasts with part of the wing still attached. Slice each breast about a third of the way from the thicker top, so the two "halves" are about even. If any spiny ribs are protruding, I use kitchen shears or a paring knife to trim them. Now you've got eight pieces of chicken, ready to cook as you wish.

# Wood-Fired Winter Sides

Use your fireplace, wood stove, grill, or fire pit to lend slow-cooked, smoky richness to these otherwise simple vegetable dishes. Of course, you can also use your oven.

## ROASTED CAULIFLOWER
### WITH OLIVES & RED PEPPER FLAKES

**SERVES 6**

1 small head of cauliflower

3 tablespoons olive oil

½ teaspoon crushed red pepper flakes

Salt and black pepper

⅓ cup pitted kalamata olives

Grated zest and juice of 1 small lemon

¼ cup torn fresh parsley leaves

Prep your grill (see page 51), fire pit, or other wood fire or preheat the oven to 425°F.

Break the cauliflower head into florets. Toss the florets in a medium bowl with the olive oil and red pepper flakes and season with salt and black pepper to taste. Transfer to an ovenproof skillet, preferably cast iron, and sprinkle the olives on top. Put the pan on the grill grates or roast in the oven until the cauliflower is tender but not mushy, 8 to 10 minutes.

Remove from the heat and toss with the lemon zest and juice and parsley. Serve straight from the skillet.

# CIDER-BRAISED BRUSSELS SPROUTS

**SERVES 6**

3 strips of bacon, cut into ¼-inch pieces

2 tablespoons olive oil

1½ pounds Brussels sprouts, halved lengthwise

Salt and pepper

⅓ cup apple cider

4 tablespoons (½ stick) unsalted butter

Prep your grill (see page 51), fire pit, or other wood fire or preheat the oven to 475°F.

Cook the bacon over medium heat in a large ovenproof skillet, preferably cast iron. Remove the bacon, blot on paper towels, and roughly chop.

Drain the bacon fat from the skillet but don't wash the pan. Add the olive oil and heat over high heat. Add the Brussels sprouts, season with salt and pepper to taste, and cook for 4 minutes.

Pour in the cider to deglaze the pan, toss in the bacon and butter, and transfer the skillet to the grill or oven. Cook for 2 minutes. Serve straight from the skillet.

Nanny—my mom's mother—made these cookies for every family gathering. I would circle the dining room credenza, where they lay piled high on a platter, moving cautiously so my mother wouldn't notice that I'd snuck about a dozen of them before the day was through. When I got older, I begged for the recipe, intent to know the secret behind their soft, chewy centers and sugar-encrusted exteriors. Time after time, I was denied. It was years later, after my grandmother passed, that I received a stack of recipe cards tagged "From Nanny, with Love." Tucked among the Broccoli Casserole, Seafood Newburg, and Baked Stuffed Shrimp recipes was the one I'd been dreaming about. I've added candied ginger for my own personal twist, but the rest is a true Nanny original. From me, with love.

MAKES ABOUT 2 DOZEN COOKIES

# Nanny's Molasses Cookies
WITH CANDIED GINGER

In a medium bowl, combine the flour, baking soda, ground ginger, cinnamon, and cloves.

In a stand mixer fitted with the paddle attachment or in a large bowl with a wooden spoon, beat together the shortening and sugar until light and fluffy. Add the eggs one at a time, incorporating each one fully before adding the next, then mix in the molasses. Add the dry ingredients to the bowl and blend until the dough just comes together. Stir in the candied ginger. Punch the dough down in the bowl with your fists so it's packed tightly at the bottom of the bowl and any air bubbles have been removed. Cover with plastic wrap and refrigerate for 30 minutes.

Preheat the oven to 375°F. Line a baking sheet with parchment.

3½ cups all-purpose flour

2 teaspoons baking soda

2 teaspoons ground ginger

1¼ teaspoons ground cinnamon

1 teaspoon ground cloves

1 cup shortening

2 cups sugar, plus more for coating the cookies

2 large eggs, beaten

½ cup molasses

⅔ cup chopped candied ginger

Using a cookie scoop, a spoon, or just your hands, form roughly 1-inch balls of dough. Roll the balls in sugar and arrange on the baking sheet, spacing them 2 inches apart. Gently press the top of each ball to flatten slightly.

Bake the cookies until cracks just begin to form on the surface, 8 to 10 minutes. The cookies will look underdone. Let them rest on the baking sheet for 2 minutes, then use a spatula to transfer them to a cooling rack to cool completely.

## Milk and Honey

Every year the first bout of cold weather strikes me as refreshing—a natural and welcome progression of the changing seasons—and I hope that New England winters as we've known them might still exist. I look forward to the first flurry of snowflakes, the ponds freezing over, and any excuse to curl up next to a roaring fireplace. I remind myself to embrace these romantic thoughts of winter because come late February, I'm sure I'll have a more frigid outlook. Until then, I stay warm and well with these recipes of milk and honey to soften, soothe, and comfort on chilly days.

## A GLASS OF WARM MILK

SERVES 1

1 cup whole milk

1 tablespoon raw honey

Pinch of grated nutmeg

Combine the milk, honey, and nutmeg in a small saucepan and warm over low heat. Take care not to scald the milk, removing it just as tiny bubbles form along the edges of the milk and it's warm, but not hot, to the touch. Sip and dream sweetly.

## A MILK & HONEY BODY SCRUB

To soften and moisturize, rub this over rough parts in the shower before rinsing off (the oil will make the floor of the shower a bit slick, so be careful). Makes enough to last through the winter or to wrap as a gift.

MAKES 1 PINT

½ cup honey

½ cup raw sugar

¼ cup powdered milk

½ cup baby oil

1 tablespoon vitamin E

Mix together all of the ingredients and transfer to a pint jar with a lid. Store in the shower or by the tub.

**On Christmas morning,** if we were lucky, my mom would make a pudding-like baked French toast flavored with cardamom and topped with jam. I decided to take the combo a step further and turn it into an even chewier, gooier version that's more suitable for dessert than breakfast.

SERVES 8

# Bread Pudding
## WITH APRICOT & CARDAMOM

Preheat the oven to 350°F.

Combine the Sauternes and cardamom pods in a small saucepan over medium heat. Add the vanilla bean and seeds. When the liquid simmers, remove the pot from the heat. Add the dried apricots and steep until the mixture is cool and the apricots are plump, about 10 minutes. Strain the apricots from the poaching liquid (reserve the liquid to add to cocktails or drizzle over ice cream) and roughly chop them.

Butter a 9-inch square baking dish with 1 tablespoon of the butter. Put the cubed bread in the dish.

Whisk together the eggs, cream, milk, granulated sugar, vanilla, cinnamon, ground cardamom, salt, and reserved apricots in a large bowl until smooth. Pour the mixture over the cubed bread and allow it to soak for 15 minutes.

Dot the remaining 3 tablespoons butter on top of the bread mixture. Bake until the top is browned and the pudding is moist but cooked through (a cake tester inserted in the center comes out clean), about 45 minutes.

Cut the warm pudding into squares and serve with a drizzle of maple syrup, a dusting of confectioners' sugar, and whipped cream.

2 cups Sauternes or other sweet dessert white wine

1 tablespoon cardamom pods

1 vanilla bean, split lengthwise and scraped

1 cup dried apricots

4 tablespoons (½ stick) unsalted butter

6 (2-inch-thick) slices of good day-old white bread, like crusty French sourdough or brioche, cubed

4 large eggs

3½ cups heavy cream

½ cup whole milk

½ cup granulated sugar

2 teaspoons vanilla extract

½ teaspoon ground cinnamon

¼ teaspoon ground cardamom

¼ teaspoon salt

Maple syrup

Confectioners' sugar

Perfectly Whipped Cream (page 62)

**This one dates back to my days** working the Fryolator at the diner. But of course I wouldn't just give you a recipe for plain-Jane fried dough. I elevate this country fair staple by adding ricotta to the batter and serving the fritters with a dollop of seasonal preserves and a tableside drizzle of vanilla custard sauce.

**MAKES ABOUT 1 DOZEN FRITTERS**

# Ricotta Fritters
## WITH CUSTARD SAUCE & PRESERVES

¾ cup all-purpose flour

2 teaspoons baking powder

½ teaspoon ground cinnamon

½ teaspoon grated nutmeg

½ teaspoon salt

Grated zest and juice of 1 lemon

1 cup fresh ricotta (ideally the thicker basket-weave variety)

2 large eggs

3 tablespoons granulated sugar

2 teaspoons vanilla extract

Vegetable oil, for frying

Confectioners' sugar

Custard Sauce (page 242)

Fruit preserves

Combine the flour, baking powder, cinnamon, nutmeg, salt, and lemon zest in a large bowl.

In a separate bowl, gently stir together the ricotta, eggs, granulated sugar, vanilla, and lemon juice. Gently whisk in the dry ingredients until just combined.

Heat oil in a deep fryer to 375°F or, alternatively, heat 2 inches of oil in a heavy-bottomed pan to the same temperature. (You can test if the oil is ready by dropping a small blob of batter into it; the batter should bubble and then brown within 30 to 40 seconds.) Choose a dish large enough to hold the fritters in a single layer and line it with paper towels.

Working in batches, drop heaping tablespoons of the batter into the oil, 6 to 8 fritters at a time. Fry the fritters, turning them frequently, until golden brown and cooked through, about 4 minutes. Transfer to the prepared dish and sprinkle with confectioners' sugar. Serve with the custard sauce and fruit preserves.

# CUSTARD SAUCE

This process is identical to that of making the base for an ice cream. As with a simple syrup, you can easily infuse this custard base with any flavor—lemon, ginger, rosemary, basil, Earl Grey, or, as here, classic vanilla. Simply omit the vanilla in this recipe, add whichever flavoring you like, and steep long enough for it to infuse, usually about 20 minutes. Serve as a custard sauce or freeze in an ice cream machine for a frozen treat.

In a medium saucepan, combine the milk, cream, sugar, salt, and vanilla bean and seeds. Bring the mixture to a simmer over medium heat. Turn off the heat and let the mixture steep for 20 minutes for the flavor to infuse.

Whisk the yolks in a medium bowl; then, still whisking, add a few tablespoons of the hot cream mixture to temper. Continue whisking as you slowly add the rest of the hot cream. Return the mixture to the saucepan and cook over medium heat, whisking constantly, until it thickens slightly but does not boil, about 4 minutes. Pour the mixture through a sieve to remove any curdled bits and refrigerate until cool. Serve cold or at room temperature.

MAKES ABOUT 4 CUPS

2 cups whole milk

2 cups heavy cream

½ cup sugar

Pinch of salt

1 vanilla bean, split lengthwise and scraped

8 large egg yolks

Not only is this dessert super-impressive and delicious, it's also the ultimate make-ahead dish. It's a simple mousse base—which you can flavor every which way from orange to pumpkin to plain vanilla—layered in a loaf pan with nut brittle, then frozen and sliced. And I highly recommend making a double batch of the brittle so you can keep some in the pantry for ice cream sundaes, yogurt, or snacking right out of the bag.

**SERVES 8**

# Frozen Lemon Terrine
## WITH PISTACHIO BRITTLE

**FOR THE BRITTLE**

1 tablespoon unsalted butter, plus more for the pan

1 cup sugar

½ cup corn syrup

½ teaspoon baking soda

1 cup pistachios, toasted

½ teaspoon Maldon salt

**FOR THE MOUSSE**

5 large egg yolks

1 cup sugar

Grated zest and juice of 2 lemons

5 large egg whites

Pinch of salt

2 cups heavy cream

1 teaspoon vanilla extract

**MAKE THE BRITTLE:** Grease a baking sheet with butter.

Clip a candy thermometer to the side of a heavy-bottomed pot. Combine the sugar, corn syrup, and ½ cup water in the pot and bring to a boil over medium heat. When the thermometer reads 330°F (the mixture will be bubbling and turning caramel-colored), remove the pot from the heat and immediately stir in the butter, baking soda, and pistachios. The mixture will bubble furiously, so be careful, but continue to stir, making sure it's well blended. Working quickly, pour the candy onto the prepared baking sheet and spread it out in a thin, even layer using a heatproof spatula. Sprinkle with the Maldon salt, then allow it to cool and harden. Break the brittle into pieces with your hands and coarsely chop.

**MAKE THE MOUSSE:** Prepare a 9 × 5-inch loaf pan by lining it with plastic wrap, leaving a 6-inch overhang on all four sides.

In the bottom of a double boiler, bring a couple inches of water to a simmer. (Or set a large heatproof bowl atop a saucepan of simmering water.) Fill a large bowl with ice water.

Combine the egg yolks, ½ cup of the sugar, and lemon zest and juice in the double boiler (or the bowl). Whip on low with a hand mixer or a whisk until the mixture becomes frothy, about 3 minutes. Set the top of the double boiler (or the bowl) in the ice bath and beat the yolk mixture on high until it becomes pale and thick, about 8 minutes. Remove from the ice bath.

In a stand mixer fitted with the whisk attachment, whip the egg whites on high speed until stiff. Slowly pour in the remaining ½ cup granulated sugar and a pinch of salt and continue to beat until incorporated.

In the clean bowl of a stand mixer or whisking by hand in a large bowl, whip the heavy cream and vanilla on high until stiff peaks form. Gently fold the whipped cream into the yolk mixture. Then fold in the egg white mixture.

Spread half of the mousse in the prepared loaf pan and sprinkle it with the brittle. Spread the remaining mousse on top and pull the plastic overhangs up and over to form a seal. Freeze the terrine until firm, at least 4 hours.

To serve, unmold, unwrap, and slice 1 to 1½ inches thick.

**This dessert will fulfill all of your chocolate dreams.** It's creamy and sexy and decadent, and people just go nuts for it. It's so rich that you want just a sliver, so you could get as many as twelve servings out of a pie. Definitely serve it with Salted Caramel Whipped Cream (page 249).

MAKES 1 (9-INCH) PIE; SERVES 10 TO 12

# Chocolate Tart
## WITH CHOCOLATE WAFER CRUST

Preheat the oven to 350°F.

**MAKE THE CRUST:** In a food processor, pulse the chocolate wafers and sugar until well ground (it's okay to have some larger bits of chocolate crumbs). Transfer the wafer mixture to a medium bowl and stir in the melted butter until well incorporated.

Press the crust mixture into a 9-inch tart pan with a removable bottom. Bake until the crust is set, about 10 minutes. Let cool completely.

**MAKE THE FILLING:** Put the chocolate chips in a large bowl.

Heat the cream in a small saucepan over medium heat until it just comes to a boil. Pour the cream over the chocolate bits and let the mixture sit for 1 minute to melt. Stir gently until the mixture is smooth.

In a separate bowl, lightly beat the eggs and vanilla. Whisk the egg mixture into the chocolate mixture until smooth, then pour the filling into the cooled tart shell.

Bake the tart just until the edges begin to puff and the first crack appears—the center will still be jiggly—18 to 20 minutes. Let cool completely, until set.

FOR THE CRUST

1 (15-ounce) box of chocolate wafers, such as Nabisco

¼ cup sugar

6 tablespoons unsalted butter, melted

FOR THE FILLING

1 cup bittersweet chocolate chips

1¼ cups heavy cream

2 large eggs

1 teaspoon vanilla extract

FOR THE GLAZE

⅓ cup bittersweet chocolate chips

¼ cup heavy cream

½ teaspoon Maldon salt

**MAKE THE GLAZE:** Put the chocolate chips in a small bowl.

In a small saucepan, heat the cream until it simmers gently and then pour it over the chocolate. Let sit for 1 minute, then whisk until smooth. Pour over the tart and allow to set, about 20 minutes. Sprinkle with Maldon salt.

Cut the tart into thin slices and serve.

**My mom worked long days as a teacher,** so during the week she didn't have a lot of time to cook. She wasn't afraid to whip out a box of gingerbread mix to make for dessert—though she'd always make her own whipped cream. This from-scratch recipe, an ode to those from-the-pantry favorites in our house, includes fresh and dried ginger and has an almost steamed pudding–like consistency.

SERVES 8

# Gingerbread
## WITH SALTED CARAMEL WHIPPED CREAM

16 tablespoons (2 sticks) unsalted butter, plus more for the pan

2½ cups all-purpose flour, plus more for the pan

2 tablespoons minced fresh ginger

1 cup boiling water

2 teaspoons baking soda

2 teaspoons ground ginger

1 teaspoon ground cinnamon

½ teaspoon ground cloves

2 teaspoons salt

½ cup packed light brown sugar

1 large egg

1 cup molasses

Salted Caramel Whipped Cream (opposite)

Preheat the oven to 350°F. Butter and flour a 9-inch square baking dish.

Add the fresh ginger to the boiling water and let steep for 15 to 20 minutes.

In a large bowl, whisk together the flour, baking soda, ground ginger, cinnamon, cloves, and salt.

In a stand mixer fitted with the paddle attachment, beat the butter and brown sugar on high speed until very light and fluffy, about 5 minutes (though I've been known to let it go for 10 to 15 if I'm multitasking). Add the egg, beat until fully incorporated, then mix in the molasses. Using a rubber spatula, gently stir in the dry ingredients by hand until just incorporated. Add the hot water and ginger and mix just until smooth.

Pour the batter into the prepared pan, smooth the top, and bake until a cake tester or knife inserted in the center comes out clean, about 45 minutes.

Let the gingerbread cool slightly before slicing into squares. Serve topped with salted caramel whipped cream.

# SALTED CARAMEL WHIPPED CREAM

I actually wasn't the one to discover the miracle that is salted caramel whipped cream. It was Ashley, who worked nights at the restaurant after farming all day. I came down to the prep kitchen one evening to find her, exhausted and zombie-like, eating what looked like a fluffy pudding straight out of the bowl. She'd taken a jar of the caramel sauce my son and I had made as Christmas gifts and folded it into whipped cream. It was easily the most delicious thing I'd tasted in a long time.

In a small heavy-bottomed saucepan, combine the sugar with 2 tablespoons water. Cook over high heat until the sugar turns golden brown, 4 to 5 minutes.

Reduce the heat to low and slowly and carefully (the mixture will bubble up) add the butter, whisking constantly. Slowly drizzle in ⅔ cup of the cream while whisking, mixing until the butter is melted and the caramel is smooth. Remove from the heat and whisk in the salt. Allow to cool completely.

Using a hand mixer, stand mixer, or whisk, whip the remaining 2 cups cream to hold firm peaks. Fold in the cooled caramel.

MAKES ABOUT 3 CUPS

½ cup sugar

2 tablespoons unsalted butter

2⅔ cups heavy cream

½ teaspoon Maldon salt

# Acknowledgments

*Many thanks:*

To the women of TLK, who bring so much love to the table each and every day. Your beauty, grace, and grit inspire me infinitely.

To Kristy, Dave, Holly, and Mom, aka "my posse." You have been steadfast in having my back despite the odds against me. Thank you for never giving up on me, eternally believing in me, and pushing me forward each day. I love you and owe you all the world.

To Jaim. Your endless love and compassion for the world around you inspires me each and every day. You have taught me so much and opened my eyes. I love you to the moon and back!

To Dad. I know we don't see eye to eye and maybe we never will, but I still have hope that eventually we will find our way. Thank you for introducing me to my everlasting love for food. That diner of yours schooled me, and I am all the better for it.

To Michael. My constant cheerleader. X

To Tony and Sally Grassi, for believing in second chances.

To Janis Donnaud, for pushing me, protecting me, pulling me up and propelling me forward. I am grateful.

To Rachel Holtzman for keeping me in line and on time! You are a lifelong friend.

To Rica Allannic for taking the chance on a girl from the middle of nowhere. To Danielle Deschenes for bringing these pages alive with grace and simplicity. To Ada Yonenaka and Kim Tyner for helping to shepherd them.

To Nicole Franzen, Chelsea Zimmer, and Kate Jordan. Our time together working on this book was pure magic. I want to relive it all over again! Missing those trout pond dips and blueberry field picnic eves with you. You will always have a place in Maine and in my heart.

*You can't make good food without good ingredients:*

To the farmers and artists who have supplied us over the years. With love and appreciation:

VILLAGE SIDE FARM
DOROLENNA FARM
MORRILL CENTURY FARM
NEW BEAT FARM
BROWNE CO. TRADING
CALDWELL FARM
FINE LINE FARM
AFTER THE FALL FARM
HAHN'S END CHEESE
LAKIN'S GORGES CHEESE
APPLETON CREAMERY
GARDENER'S HONEY
HELEN TIRONE & HER MOST
    AMAZING HEIRLOOM TOMATOES
CROOKED FACED CREAMERY
MOODYTOWN GARDENS
HUBBARD BROOK FARM
RISING UP FARM
PEACEMEAL FARM
COMMONWEALTH POULTRY CO.
TINDER HEARTH
44 NORTH COFFEE
BELLADONNA FLOWER FARM
MEGHAN FLYNN CERAMICS

# Index

(Page references in italics refer to illustrations.)

Honey: grilled stone fruit, blue cheese
and, 128
honeyed hot toddy with thyme, 147
milk and honey body scrub, 238
and plum pie, rustic, with vanilla
bean soured cream, 178–79
warm milk with, 238
Horseradish-beetroot flavored ice, 208
Horseradish mayo, 37
Hot dogs: classic clam boil, 115
Hot toddy, honeyed, with thyme, 147

## I

Ice: beetroot-horseradish flavored,
208
ripe cantaloupe and ruby port, 138
Ice cream: custard base for, 242
sundae, maple and candied walnut,
76–77

## K

Kale Caesar, with skillet croutons and
duck egg, 199

## L

Lamb, wood-smoked leg of, with
garlic scape and mint pesto, 56–57
Lavender: lavender frites, 120
lavender sink scrub, 59
skillet mussels with rosemary, lime
and, 107
Lemon(s): lemon chive mayo, 37
roasted lemon and rosemary, cast-
iron chicken with, 232
shrimp stew with toasted fennel,
chives and, 55
terrine, frozen, with pistachio
brittle, 244–45
vodka infused with, 147
Lentils: fried potato and warm lentil
salad, 231
Lime, skillet mussels with rosemary,
lavender and, 107
Lobster, 11-minute, 102–3, 209

## M

Maine shrimp roll, 52
Manhattan, maple, 144
Maple syrup, 80
maple and candied walnut ice
cream sundae, 76–77
maple Manhattan, 144
Margarita, cider and cilantro, spicy,
146
Mascarpone and hazelnuts, sweet
parsnip cake with, 74–75
Mayo, homemade, 37

Meatloaf, Dad's, with parsnip puree
and root cellar slaw, 225–26
Meats, 58. *See also specific types*
basic brine for, 170
Mignonette sauce, 208
Milk and honey body scrub, 238
Milk, warm, with honey, 238
Mint: and garlic scape pesto, 57
spring bread salad with asparagus,
radishes, peas and, 28
Mojito, blackberry and basil, 145
Molasses cookies, Nanny's, with
candied ginger, 236–37
Moose stew with parsley dumplings,
175–76
Mousse, chicken liver, 195
Mushroom toast, warm, with port,
herbs and ricotta, 158
Mussels, 108
skillet, with rosemary, lavender, and
lime, 107
Mustard vinaigrette, fried rabbit or
duck with charred radicchio and,
165–66

## N

Napkins, handmade, 227
Nasturtiums, 113
Needhams, parsnip, 68
New England brown bread, 219
New England dinner, corned brisket,
220
Nutmeg custard, sweet, 184
Nuts, candied, 77

## O

Olive oil, 18
and anchovy dip, warm, 194
Olives: roasted cauliflower with red
pepper flakes and, 234
tapenade, 112
warmed, 153
Oysters: fried, with root cellar slaw
and horseradish mayonnaise, 202
on the half shell, 204–5
toppings for raw oysters, 208

## P

Pans, 18–19
Parsley dumplings, moose stew with,
175–76
Parsnip(s): cake, sweet, with hazelnuts
and mascarpone, 74–75
crispy parsnip ribbons, 152
parsnip Needhams, 68
puree, 226
spring-dug-parsnip hash, 45

Peach(es): and ginger cobbler, 137
grilled, pork burgers with bacon,
blue cheese and, 122
grilled stone fruit, blue cheese and,
honey, 128
Pears: caramelized pear and cornmeal
skillet cake, 185–86
Peas, spring bread salad with
asparagus, radishes, mint and, 28
Pepper, black, 18
Periwinkles in a skillet with garlic and
parsley, 27
Pesto, garlic scape and mint, 57
Pie: graham cracker, 67
rustic plum and honey, with vanilla
bean soured cream, 178–79
spiced squash chiffon, 188–89
Pistachio brittle, frozen lemon terrine
with, 244–45
Plum(s): grilled stone fruit, blue
cheese and honey, 128
and honey pie, rustic, with vanilla
bean soured cream, 178–79
Poison ivy soother, 99
Poppy seed buns, 123
Pork. *See also* Bacon; Sausage(s)
burgers, with grilled peaches, bacon
and blue cheese, 122
and chicken liver terrine, 197–98
chops, rosemary-brined, with
apples, potatoes and brandy,
169–70
Dad's meatloaf with parsnip puree
and root cellar slaw, 225–26
picnic shoulder, slow-roasted, with
cinnamon and rosemary, 171
Port: cantaloupe and ruby port ice,
138
warm mushroom toast with herbs,
ricotta and, 158
Potatoes: classic clam boil, 115
corned brisket New England dinner,
220
fried potato and warm lentil salad,
231
lavender frites, 120
Maine halibut Niçoise, 111–12
perfect potato salad, 106
rosemary-brined pork chops
with apples, brandy and,
169–70
Prosecco-cider cocktail, 146

## Q

Quail eggs and celery salt, 24